Seeker Dreamer:
Amazing, Brilliant, Compassionate YOU

authorHOUSE®

AuthorHouse™LLC
1663 Liberty Drive
Bloomington, IN 47403
www.authorhouse.com
Phone: 1-800-839-8640

Published by AuthorHouse   09/30/2013

ISBN: 978-1-4918-1646-2 (sc)

Photography Credits

Tyrone Rasheed
Front Cover---Frog on a Lily pad
Back Cover Photo of Melony McGant
Sunset on Water, Section---Releasing Limitations, page 139
Daisy close up, Section---Rediscovering Joy, page 59
Daisies, Section---Trusting the Need NOT to Control, page 179
Bell Flower, Section--- Integrity and Courage, page 219

Melony McGant
Heart in Sand, page 199

Other photos
Stockphotography

Seeker Dreamer: Amazing, Brilliant, Compassionate YOU

By Reverend Melony McGant

A JOURNAL WORKBOOK FOR SELF-DISCOVERY
AND EMPOWERMENT

Dedication

50 years ago, I was blessed to attend the Historic March on Washington on August 28th, 1963 with my mother, Betty J. Tilman, a Dreamer Civil Rights Foot Soldier, Peace and Freedom, Free South Africa activist and community volunteer who lives in Pittsburgh, Pennsylvania.

This book is my gift to her in celebration of her 80th birthday. Because of her compassion and wisdom, I was nurtured as a dreamer and grew up believing that the dream of Dr. Martin Luther King, Jr. and all those who desired equity, freedom and Love for Humanity was my dream too. It remains my dream for **all** our children; not just in the United States but throughout every nation of the world. I will always believe that we have the potential to live our collective greatness through compassion and Love!

I am also fortunate to count many Seeker Dreamers among my mentors and supporters including James E. Aloway, Deborah Ballard, Ted Bennett, John and Gloria Brown, John Butler, Wilhemina Byrd Brown, Byrd R. Brown Esq., Bill Blakey, Dewitt Bolden, Ida Campbell, Stevens Jay Carter, Gayle Hodnett Dobbs, Katherine Dunham, Marcia L. Dyson, Alma Speed Fox, Sedrick Gardner, Sunil Gupta, Mary Gloster, Sylvia Golbin Goodman, Elizabeth Hin, Luddy Hayden, James Henry, Warrington Hudlin, Helena and John Hughes, Dr. Donald and Bebe Henderson, Oliver Isaac, Maida Springer Kemp, Virginia McGant, Congressman Parren Mitchell, Daniel Mujahid, Darcia Mitchell, Joyce Morrow Jones, Jackie Mullins, Dr. Sandra Murray, Tyrone and Barbara Rasheed, Mohamed Rum, Gabbi Russell, Dolores Stanton, Barbara Davis White, Dr. Glory Van Scott, Reginald Yates and many more not named but remembered in my heart.

For Them, YOU and Every Seeker Dreamer Ascended, Living or Destined to Be Born... May Love Be Our Motivation!

We will be more likely to Prosper Collectively when we decide that Compassion has meaning and is useful in Today's World!

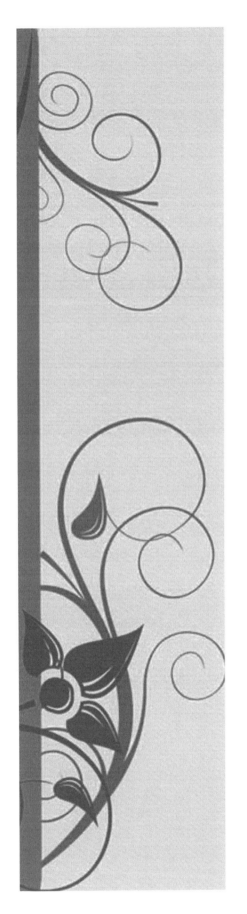

Dreams

What if the dreams
of our hearts
materialize only
when we walk with
patience, grace and love?

What if we are given
the wisdom of the Ancients
through our dreams
and must believe it
to live them?

What if peace lies
within the framework
of the dream?
Wake Up Dreamer,
and live the dream.

Contents

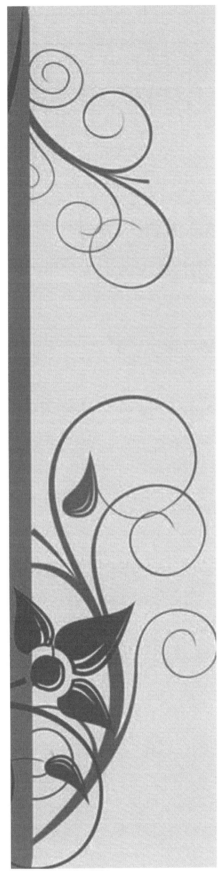

FOREWARD

By Dr. Glory Van Scott

Reverend Melony McGant
In writing this Journal Workbook
Takes You, on a Journey
Down a powerful open path,
Where YOU,--the "Seeker, Dreamer,"
can plant your feet,
leaving footsteps (imprints) for
others to follow.

Reverend McGant, gives you
an unusual, finely tuned
Spiritual educational
footprint map to lead you
to the Borders of your
clear destiny —
into your Border
and Beyond the Borders
of your Destiny
and its traveling guide,
—Your Imagination.

If your eyes are closed
to the words of Reverend McGant,
then, you see "nothing".
If your ears are closed
to the messages of Reverend McGant
barring you from hearing them
riding in on the breath
of a Spring breeze,
then you hear "nothing".

And if your heart, mind and soul
are closed to the writing
of Reverend McGant,
then, you might feel
the convoluted, deflated Blossom
of "Nothing".

But, I trust that you will
Embrace the words,
values and message in
Reverend McGant's Journal Workbook
SEEKER DREAMER,

And as she says,
"Become the Amazing, Brilliant,
Compassionate YOU!"

. . . .

About Dr. Glory Van Scott

Dr. Glory Van Scott is a producer/director, actress, singer, dancer, composer, playwright and Founder of Dr. Glory's Youth Theatre which operates in Riverside Church Theatre.

For 10 years, Dr. Van Scott was Professor of Theatre at Bucknell University's Pennsylvania Governor's School for the Arts, and later taught at Fordham University. She holds a PhD. from Antioch Union Graduate School, with Undergraduate Degrees MA, BA, from Goddard College.

Dr. Van Scott has performed on and off-Broadway & television. She was the Rolls Royce Lady in the film, *The Wiz*, and has toured all over the world. She is a former principal dancer with the Katherine Dunham, Agnes De Mille, and Talley Beatty Companies, and was a member of the American Ballet Theatre.

Dr. Glory Van Scott is also a recipient of an Eleanor Roosevelt N.A.I.R.O. grant in the field of Human Relations and a Breadloaf Writers Scholar. She has produced and composed more than twenty five musicals, including the critically acclaimed *"Miss Truth"*, directed and choreographed by Louis Johnson. Her much anticipated biography, *"GLORY: A Memoir Salute"* will be available in June, 2014.

Special Thanks from Melony

I want to acknowledge and give special thanks to two people whose creative talent and gifts have contributed to this workbook journal:

To Seeker Dreamer Workbook Visionary, graphic artist and editor, Joyce Morrow Jones.

Joyce had the inspiration for me to compile my meditations in a journal workbook format. I appreciate her as and editor. It was an added plus that she also does book layout, information and graphic design. She has done a beautiful job in interpreting the structure of the meditations for the Seeker Dreamer.

Joyce has many talents, of particular note, she is a folk artist specializing in doll art reflecting many cultural and esoteric representations of spiritual icons.

To Tyrone Rasheed for his creative photography!

Tyrone provided the images for the Front and Back Cover Photos as well as several images within the journal workbook. He and his wife Barbara have been my dear friends for more than 25 years. The cover photo of the frog on the lily pad gave birth to a meditation and serves as inspiration for this journal workbook.

As well, Joyce was enchanted by the conceptual image as well, because as she states, *"the frog is not inactive; but, rather in its stillness, there is meditation and readiness."*

Tyrone Rasheed, Artist Statement

I've been given this gift of photography from God. I love documenting moments in the lives of people. My images of family days, birthdays, weddings, retirement parties, births, funerals and family portraits will live on forever. I live, eat, and sleep photography. I'm living my dream doing what I love every time I use my camera.

For more information or to hire, New York City Based photographer Tyrone Rasheed contact him at tyronerasheed7@gmail.com or call 212-491-2891

From the Editor

It starts with the Breath ...

That's how I met Melony by way of her meditations posted to Facebook. So it is no surprise that Facebook has become her ministry of love, reaching out to many who will only know her through the energy of LOVE. I came across her meditations in a group and was taken aback with pause as she encouraged the reader to "breathe" throughout each posted meditation. I reflected that my breathing is often shallow throughout the day, so the daily reminders became essential to "stopping", and in that stillness ... to breathe.

> Breathing is something we do without much thought. We take it for granted, but when we begin each moment with the breath, we have the opportunity to exist with the energy of the Divine Creator; and, even more importantly, to fulfill our destiny while living with purpose.

> Many spiritual traditions teach about breathing - deep meditative breathing. The inhalation and exhalation of energy which flows within us and sustains us. Breathing IS transformative. With each exchange, we can shift and alter the energy around us - experiencing peace where anger was present. Acheiving harmony where discord was looming large. Sending out waves of love in instances where sorrow filled hearts with hopelessness.

I have truly enjoyed the process of reviewing Melony's words of inspiration compiled for this workbook journal. In our first conversation together, it was like a mutual admiration session with both of us resonating with the other's inspirational writings. The more we talked, the more I was convinced that her next book should be "instructional" to guide seekers on the journey.

So, here is your invitation:

> *Read the meditations*
> *Reflect on the personal application*
> *Be still and breathe*
> *Meditate on the spiritual resonance*
> *Create your affirmations*
> *Journal your process*

and... then repeat the process as you move throughout the journal workbook.

Even though there are journal sections, there is not a predefined sequence. Let your heart and spirit guide you through the process towards becoming Amazing, Brilliant, Compassionate YOU!

Joyce Morrow Jones
Editor & Graphic Designer

From Melony - An Introduction

On planes, trains, buses & automobiles; through concrete deserts, sandy beaches, red dirt plains and mountain hills, I have searched for the me I lost somewhere striving for the American Dream; Or, what I thought was the American Dream. In my attempts to discover my passion, I found that I liked everything and loved nothing. As a young woman in rebellion, I grew to be manipulative, loving no one … not even myself.

Searching for money, power and success, I wanted to be a successful marketing professional. My primary goals were to have my voice heard while making a change in our society with some measure of significance. So, in pursuit of these goals – accompanied with zeal and passion, I also met resistance. Resistance soon became an useful ally – using that energy to fight the good fight. And I did.

By normal standards, while living in Pittsburgh, PA, you could say, I was successful. I owned my own business, worked hard to meet payroll weekly, helped clients achieve their marketing objectives, led workshops, planned media tours, press conferences, wrote speeches & coordinated special events. I lobbied for all the "right causes", and even some of the "wrong causes". I was known as a "brilliant rebel" driving my staff bananas by insisting that work was life's number one priority. They called the office Miss Mellie's Plantation and created a cartoon series. I laughed. Oh, how I laughed!

Pro-bono was my middle name but even with all my good community deeds, I was still a taskmaster. Inside I was dying. I was tired of fighting and wanting to belong. During this time my mom Betty J. Tilman lost her job after more than 27 years, and then endured two bouts of cancer. I became a doting daughter even though health issues were looming largely for me as well and my quality of life began slipping away.

Perhaps, I enjoyed being a martyr, though, at times, the burden was too heavy. Thinking a change would help, I prayed for financial security and less responsibility. The Universe said, "Okay". Within weeks of my request, I closed my business and took a job at a major advertising agency.

The money was good; however, the transition was extremely difficult.

Still, all was in Divine Order. A few months later I had surgery and plenty of time to reflect ... plenty of time to evaluate how, when & why I had closed my heart. I began a New Journey! Ultimately, the path I have now chosen allows me a new way of thinking about my life, my purpose and about Love. Today I marvel at the toddler that gives me a smile, or a hug and says "Hi, Miss Mellie Rainbow!".

Somewhere along the way I acknowledged the Seeker Dreamer: the sharing of the journey and life-story; the power of taking time to still myself, reflecting and breathing. Rediscovering the newness and transition of Love, friendships, and the True Potential of Our Human Collective. So, I greet you as well – Seeker Dreamer. As you begin or continue on your Journey of Hope and Purpose, I leave you with this parable...

Seeker Dreamer —

When Ego did not trust the Creator's Love, he found himself lost in perpetual storms of wrong words, actions and disappointment. It seemed like for eons, Ego forbade the Heart from experiencing joy and joined with Misery to create dis-order and hate throughout the World.

Some humans enslaved others who looked differently. They stole the precious resources and treasured legacies and fought religious wars to maintain control. For a time it appeared that this was to become the sad destiny of Earth. And the Great Mother Cried. Her tears moved hearts of a few who then felt the undercurrent of the Creator's Love and the few who had awakened from the horrible nightmare created by Ego and Misery.

Amazing, Brilliant, Compassionate YOU!

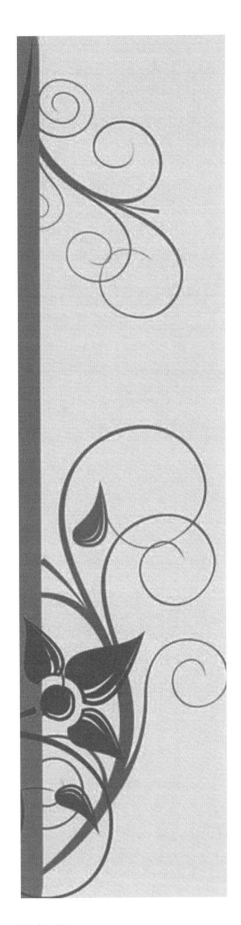

They began to Breathe Deeply and see Beauty in the Stars, in the Moon and Sun. They began to marvel at the birds song, the lives of animals and fish, and the rhythm of the winds and oceans. They learned the history of Earth-Heart through the rocks and stones. They discovered the oxygen of Love and studied the wisdom of trees. Plant life offered food and healing.

With Each Breathe they took in Love, they grew braver, and many more re-membered the Great Mother and Awakened in Love. YOU are one of the many born to honor the Creator and Rise in understanding and compassion through the Great Mother.

Breathe Deeply 10 Times. Breathe In Truth. Know there is only Love. Exhale the Nightmare Created by Ego and Misery. Now that you have Awakened, allow Divine Grace to lead your Heart. Listen to song of your Soul. It is the Creator's Song of Love.

Again, Ten Times Breathe In Love. Exhale Love. There is no turning back. The only way to heal and live and prosper on Earth-Heart is to Stay Awake Seeker Dreamer, and Trust Only Love!

You are already on the path to discovering, celebrating, and enriching the Amazing, Brilliant, Compassionate YOU!

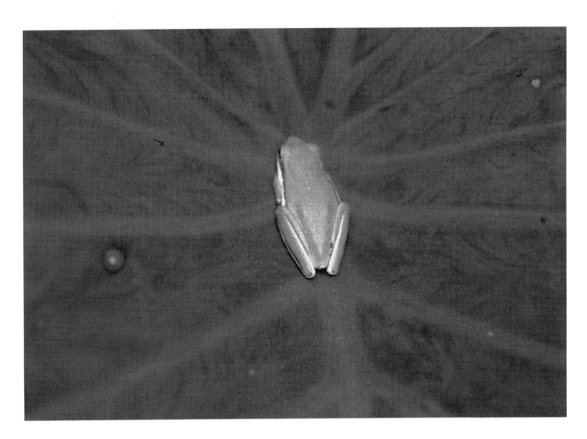

I Am a Seeker Dreamer
I Am the Frog Resting
on the Lilypad.

I Breathe deeply 10 Times.
As I prepare for my New journey,
I ask myself, "What Will I Do?"

I still my mind, open my heart and wait for
the Answer...

I Am a Seeker Dreamer, just like the Frog who rests on the Lilypad, I decide that each day I will organize the details of my life so that my mind, body and heart are in alignment.

With Courage, Fortitude and Patience, I will work vigorously to exceed my own expectations. Because balance is necessary, I will do at least two things I enjoy everyday and share joyously.

I promise myself that when Divine Spirit speaks in my heart or through others, I will listen with compassion so that I may know; and act with gentle understanding.

I Am the Frog resting on the Lilypad.
I Breathe Deeply many times as I prepare for my new journey.

Though my exact destination is unknown, I trust that as I am ready, All Will Be Revealed through Love!

I AM a Seeker Dreamer ...
I AM the frog on the lilypad.

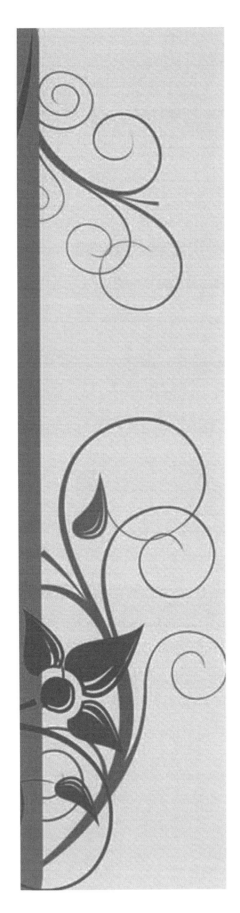

Special Thanks
to my Author House Team...

Their compassion,
good listening
and attention to detail
has created a gift
of mystery and joy
for Each of us to hold,
learn from, and Share....

Namaste,

Rev. Melony McGant

Spirit of the Dreamer

Whether or not we are aware, there is a tiny doorway waiting for each of us to step through. It is here, in this small opening of eternal light that we can rediscover hope and align ourselves with our true nature and a Divine Spirit.

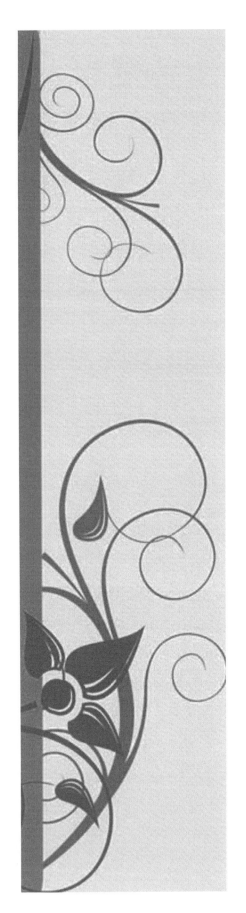

Reflections on the
Spirit of the Dreamer

. . . .

Calling All Dreamers!

We must be grateful for our dreamers. It is our collective dream of peace and our commitment to goodness moment to moment that allows us to be kind in a world that has lost its moral compass.

Today, the Uni-Verse is calling all dreamers!

Live inspired.

Offer and be your best in goodness.

Sing of hope. Embrace, believe and live the collective dream!

The Spirit of a Dreamer focuses on the spiritual ...

A Seeker Dreamer knows that the focus is on the spiritual and not material success.

The Seeker Dreamer is guided by the Spiritual and learns to use the material to Promote More Good and Challenge Evil.

Personal Material Success is empty without Love.

Be Guided to Help Make the World Better.

Use Your Voice and Material Success With Loving Respect for Justice and All Humanity!

Dreamers desire to care and be fair

When people awaken in truth, they will realize the best of life comes with sharing and love. Songs of Civil Rights will be sung and taught to children.

Dreamers will peacefully challenge broken systems of greed and call for fairness and equity!

Good Change will take time, but it will come! Keep joining together with awareness and compassion.

Dreamers, raise your voices in unity. Begin to care and be fair!

Amazing, Brilliant, Compassionate YOU!

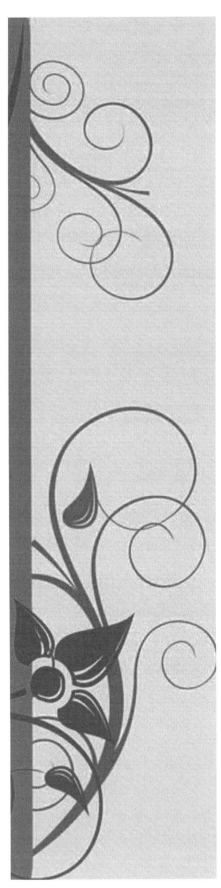

Dreamers Remember the Forgotten Familiar

When Genius and Compassion came to live among us, they did not ask to be billionaires; for they knew that greed and love of money was destroying the earth.

Genius and Compassion asked for a willingness to see the beauty in the Forgotten Familiar.

In every sunrise and sunset; in every fruit, flower and tree; in every birth, death and re-birth; through every storm or violent unnecessary war, Hope has become the Forgotten Familiar that makes it possible to live and honor the power of Abiding Love.

Remembering that Genius and Compassion live within me, I open my heart and see the beauty in the Forgotten Familiar.

Hope lives in trees and flowers and mountains and oceans. Hope grows with trust and in every child offers its smiles of Love.

To even the unworthy among us, Hope, the Forgotten Familiar is the Master Creator's constant offering of forgiveness so that we may learn to live, work and prosper together in peace with Abiding Love!

The Dreamer seeks to connect and be in harmony ...

Dreamers learn to listen and observe; honoring the diversity of ideas and seeking the commonality that resides in every heart. Living and appreciating the core values of a loving purpose, the dreamer goes deep into the depths of their own soul consciousness.

Re-membering truth the dreamer steps onto the unity bridge with a song that children desire to live and sing....

One World, One Heart, One Love!

~ • ~

Dreamers witness the prism of hope even when life is difficult with war and suffering. The people pray. Some walk believing that Good could prevail. G-d answered with a Song. Across the planet, the Song brought the Sun. People's smiles became like rainbows after generations of stormy rains.

In the Sun, dreamers hearts glistened with vibrant colors and of respect. Dreamers saw each other through the Prism of Hope and became Bright Lights singing of Love!

Amazing, Brilliant, Compassionate YOU!

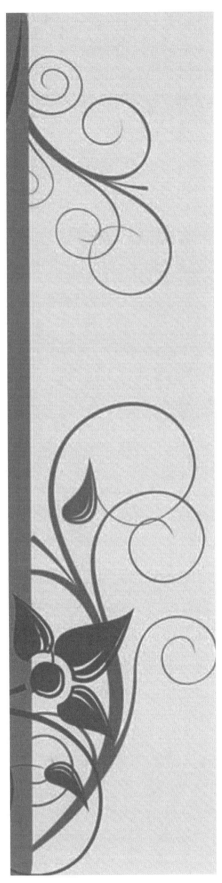

A Dreamer is not daunted by the naysayers and obstacles ...

When the Dreamer began to make good change, family and friends were angry because she stopped complaining and spent more time helping others.

"Don't be a fool! Those people don't care about you like we do. You'll lose everything!" they said."

The Dreamer thought about what they said. She knew that her dream required great sacrifice. But in her heart, she embraced her own integrity and discovered great faith.

It was then that she was able to move forward into her unknown destiny!

~ • ~

Dreamer Believers embrace The Master Creator in their hearts gladly clearing the clutter of old envy, and sweeping away disappointment.

Fear loses focus and departs when the many prayers were said by Hope.

Homes sparkled and had the fresh scent of Spring. Faith, Gratitude, Compassion, Courage, Charity,

Forgiveness, Mercy and Understanding went from house to house and became welcomed guests at every Table of Appreciation.

LOVE filled Every Home and the People began to Prosper with New Hope!

~ • ~

When my path becomes rocky with disappointment, I learn to walk carefully, with discernment.

"Just Hold On", Clear Vision and Hope say as they take my hand and lead me in Faith.

"Just Hold On! It is another beautiful day to live joyfully."

The good intention I see in others helps me to reflect more good.

Today I see the lesson of good in every circumstance and offer only good in return! Humility and Joy light the way!

~ • ~

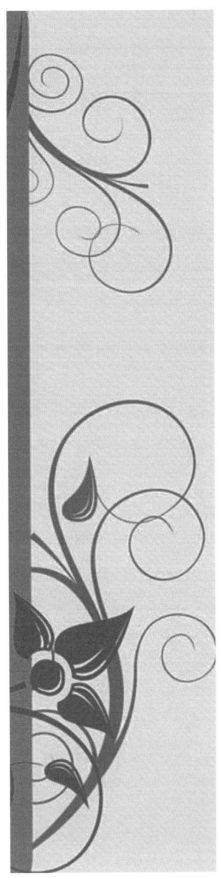

Dreamers, Do No Harm

Let us make the choice to harm none; to help many and live the way Jesus Christ lived. Dreamers awaken with gratitude.

Open your hearts with hope and forgiveness. Be inspired by Love. With Mercy and Loving Compassion, let us move forward with a commitment to joyfully honor, nurture, and support one another.

Have Faith in Good. Become the PEACE! This wish is G-D's Dream for Humanity! Blessed Be Unto YOU!

~ • ~

Beloveds, Slow down and breathe deeply. Be respectful.

Let your every action reflect your goodness and hope for the healing of our Earth-Heart.

Offer your gentle gratitude through cooperation. Dreamers, honor every child, every elder and every sentient being you see with acts of kindness.

Realign your thoughts so that you Vision and Share the Light of your Joyful Healing Heart!

The Spirit of a Dreamer Honors our Elders

When a Seeker Dreamer offers to assist and uplift the important legacy of an elder, it must NOT be for personal recognition or gain.

Our humble actions should help to create a wider understanding of the elder's gifts which the society has often ignored or forgotten.

We must Honor Our Elders, and offer respect with only good intention.

~ • ~

Amazing, Brilliant, Compassionate YOU!

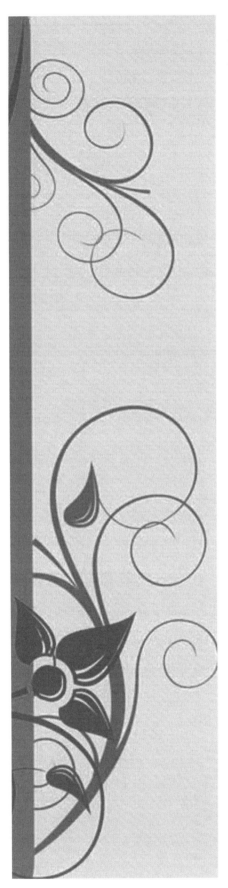

A Hopeful Dreamer desires the highest good for our children.

I can only hope that our enthusiasm and desire for goodness becomes more poignant and real each passing day. May we learn to embody mercy and compassion for all so that all are safe and free to make good choices.

May we live our lives as a good neighbors in loving prosperous communities of respect and tolerance.

May we share our time together nurturing hearts and building strong peaceful, healing foundations of hope for children to explore and grow and share their many gifts with love.

~ • ~

Dreamers desire children to grow and learn. Every day we are awakened, we are filled with the breath of creative hope by our Master MotherFatherCreator.

Our children watch, listen and learn. Be peaceful. Embrace hope and patience as wisdom and offer it to others.

This is the way our faithful, kind, creative actions bring more light into Universe.

Dreamers, be patience even in disagreement. Help our children grow to be peaceful, bright lights of hope and love!

~ • ~

Every Child Born is a Miracle of Grace. Celebrate the child of joy and wonder within others and yourselves.

Dreamers, sing your Songs of Healing Peace. Walk with Faith, Forgiveness and Mercy!
Be playful, joyful and hopeful.

Open your hearts and surely you will become like stars dancing through the Uni-Verse of Love.

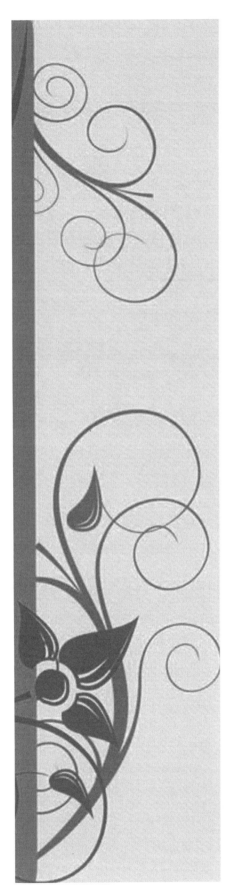

Beloved Dreamers, Let Us Live With Grace!

Thank you for your unique contributions to healing our planet. In these transitional times, it is important to feel connected to all that is, and to re-member that we are not alone.

The trees and other plant life that give us oxygen to breathe love, share joy. Birds and other animals bring us Divine messages and support. It is now that we too must find joy within our hearts and share it with others.

I know from personal experience that sometimes our gifts may be rejected. Still as we give, GRACE moves through us and gives us courage to give again, and again with more LOVE.

For many of us, the day to day concerns of life are very challenging.

Collectively, shadows of fear have gained an unusual strength, and are creating havoc on our glorious Earth=Heart.

Conflict, confusion, unnatural violence, and lack of appreciation for each other have many of us, even global leaders living in a state of anxiety.

Some are wearing fear as a second skin and causing irreparable harm. Others of us are carrying the pain and hurt of rejection. We are all beings of LOVE. It is time to release our mental swords of fear. It is time to let go of past disappointments.

As we are able to do this, JOY and innocence will move through us as a Rainbow of Grace. Whether or not we are aware, there is a tiny doorway waiting for each of us to step through. It is here, in this small opening of eternal light that we can rediscover hope and align ourselves with our true nature and a Divine Spirit.

It is time for us to organize our lives with humility, compassion, loving kindness and creativity. Right now, we each have the opportunity to re-member our inherent wisdom.

We can use our intuition by magnifying the mustard seeds of LOVE. This will allow us to share our hope and courage so that we are able to have right words, and right actions for each personal, community or global situation.

Let us each re-commit to creating a world of equity, sustainability and peace. Let our individual joy and cooperation act as beacons of light to assist others in regaining hope and experiencing healing.

Let us each believe in our own inherent goodness without a shadow of a doubt! For as we believe it — so it shall be. It is within the miracle of LOVE that crystals reflect rainbows of JOY! Let us live in the moment with appreciation, faith and hope.

Let us sing songs of compassion, walk with kindness, understanding, and a dedicated spirit of LOVE.

I ask each of you to release your personal cloaks of fear and pain into the universe.

LET THEM GO NOW.

Affirming Your Dream

Spectacular You!!!

Do you know that the Master Creator thinks you are Spectacular?
Yes, You - All of You! You wrapped in love, and learning compassion as you dream big dreams of kindness; and grow in understanding. When the beauty of your heart is constantly blossoming in humility and goodness, then you are caring and sharing with your neighbors. They are spectacular too. Together you must learn to live in Peace and Bring Good Change to the World.

Remember, You Are Spectacular!
Please, Keep Blossoming in Kindness
and Love!

Amazing, Brilliant, Compassionate YOU!

Capable and Worthy

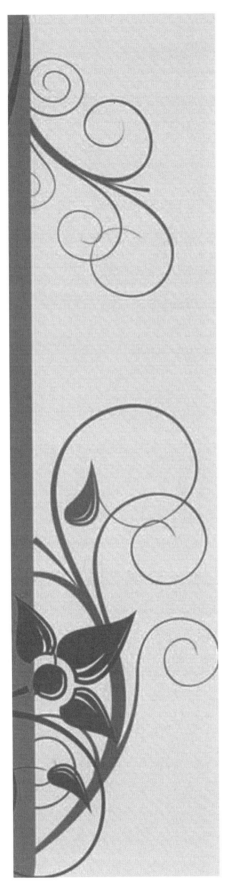

First know that you are a capable, worthy individual.

Be consistent and disciplined in your efforts as you plant new seeds and lay the groundwork for growth and opportunity.

Share your harvest and build good relationships.

Be flexible and patient as you grow and change. Risk will be required.

Start Today Dreamer.

You Are Capable and Worthy of Good Fortune!

My Life Is A Work In Progress!

My life is a work in progress. The picture painted in my heart is still incomplete.

The vibrant blues and greens and oranges show my many failures that lead way to greater successes.

The red, purple and yellow hearts remind me of all that I have lost, and each time I have fallen. Humility drew the hearts as she helped me up and taught me Love's Truth.

Compassion, Forgiveness, and Mercy teach me how to move through the tunnels of Sorrow; and know both Joy and Peace.

My life is a colorful work in progress.

It has a beautiful texture of hope; and through every storm, Faith becomes My Rainbow of Understanding!

Amazing, Brilliant, Compassionate YOU!

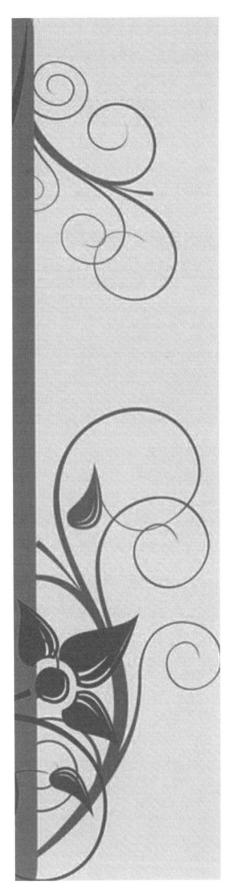

Myopic Vision

We must be careful of our Myopic Vision. What we do and how we speak has an affect on others. It's Not Always just about You!

A Seeker Dreamer walks with a cloak and heart of Integrity and honors the path of Love even while others are propelled by self interest!

Today, offer your gifts with compassion for the greater good of humanity. Allow your vision and the melody of your song to be Unselfish Love!

Being Successful

Every dreamer may experience failure of a goal but because you tried, a new door will open. Being successful means that you discover your purpose.

Today open the door of your secret temple. Look deep within your heart. Resolve to live with a loving purpose. Allow your special gifts into the world!

Speaking Truth

When you are speaking TRUTH and call for action, it triggers many hearts.

The response may not always be kind. It may be *"Leave me alone! I want to go back to sleep!"*.

Your heart will be broken many times and you will learn new lessons. Some of you will ask "Is It Worth It?".

A Seeker Dreamer Believer will ask, *"AM I Willing to Love G-d In ALL Without Expectation or Immediate Validation?"*

When your answer is "YES", your entire life will become a Loving TRUTH!

I Give Thanks

I Breathe Deeply Ten Times and clear my mind and my heart of all my preconceived notions of how life and this day should be.

I Give Thanks to the Master Creator for allowing me to be on this Earth.

I Give Thanks for waking up today; for the storms that have turned me and my life upside down; for the rainbows of hope and kindness shared by children, family, friends and the strangers who become friends.

I Give Thanks for the shining Sun of Love that teaches me to embrace our cultural differences with Joy and honor Elders with Loving Respect.

I Breathe Deeply in Gratitude for the mistakes I have made which turned out to offer important lessons of humility and taught me to have Courage to live my dreams.

I Breathe and feel the Spirit of Hope come Alive in my body and my heart.

I Give Thanks to All Creations of Love and Purpose and honor Love and Purpose within Myself.

For all that is known and for the Eternal Mystery and Answers Hidden and Discovered Only through Love, I Give Thanks!

Breathing

Today, Breathe Deeply Six Times.

In, Gratitude.

Out, Love!

Now, Be Grateful for Your Past — the good times; the hard times and the times you asked *"Why ME?"*.

There will be days when you must say goodbye, so that you can make room to Start Again.

When we live through a crisis or difficulty, a wise one learns to ask *"Why Not Me?"*. Then with humility and hope, you will feel your heart jump for joy!

Breathe Deeply and Re-Member ... Every New Day brings a new challenge so that you can grow and shine your light.

Always walk with your good friends, Gratitude and Faith, and allow Every New Day to become — the Best Yet!

Amazing, Brilliant, Compassionate YOU!

Walk In Truth

People may ignore you because of where you come from, your social status or your race. Even your birth family may choose to close their hearts to you when you have been baptized in Love.

Walk In Truth Anyway.

Truth is the only way to live as a Being of Love. Knowing, speaking and being the Truth is how we live Our Purpose.

Everyone has a purpose and a contribution to make on this planet. It is something that only You can do, or say or write in the fabric of time.

Even when it seems like all the familiar doors have closed, please don't give up.

Walk in Truth Anyway!

Your destiny lies beyond the jealous or petty. Your Destiny Resides In the Heart of Love.

Let Great Love Travel With You

Why not run, laugh, sing, and dance?
Swim in the ocean, a lake or a river.
Take a walk in the park. Sit down on
the grass and discuss life with a Tree.

Say hello to the birds and butterflies
that circle around and say "Are you
speaking to me?"

When you've lost something or
someone dear; say farewell and so
long in your heart!

Then, Dream a New Dream!

Why not plant new seeds in the
garden of your heart? Now it's time
to DO YOUR PART. Spend time with
your family, your neighbors and
friends too.

Just remember, In All You Think, Say
and Do, Let Great LOVE Travel with
YOU!

Amazing, Brilliant, Compassionate YOU!

Breathing Meditations

When you find yourself lost, Stop.

Breathe Deeply and take time to re-member
and honor your dreams.

Amazing, Brilliant, Compassionate YOU!

First, BREATHE!

When you find yourself lost, Stop.
Breathe Deeply and take time to re-member
and honor your dreams.

Ask yourself good questions.
What have you Learned?
Breathe Deeply.

What have you accomplished?
Breathe Deeply.

What have you shared?
Breathe Deeply.

What mistakes have you made?
How Must You Change?
Listen deeply.
BREATHE.

Allow your whole be-ing to absorb
the truthful answers.
BREATHE.

Listen to your heart as it speaks of JOY.
BREATHE.

Take all that you have discovered
in truth and offer Gratitude
for the gift of wisdom in your Life.
BREATHE.

Now, with courage, integrity and tenacity,
begin with JOY to re-route your journey!

First, BREATHE!

OASIS OF POSSIBILITY

Through the rains of change and sand storms of growth I have traveled through my mind and entered the Uni-Verse of my heart.

Intuition has led me through deserts of mystery until we arrived at the Oasis of Possibility. Through this experience, I have learned also to take the hands of my Friends, Trust and Courage.

Today, I Breathe Deeply Ten Times.
I Inhale Patience.
I Exhale a Desire for Good Change.
I Breathe and Breathe.

I ask My Dear Friends, Intuition, Trust and Courage to join me. Together we offer hopeful Prayers of Gratitude.

With Patience, we prepare to journey once again to the Oasis of Possibility!

First, We Breathe!

Amazing, Brilliant, Compassionate YOU!

FOREVER ONE

I Breathe Deeply Six Times and imagine that we
are One in Our Creator's Heart. I Breathe and
feel, and watch and listen to the Earth's Song.

A sun/son returns,
a daughter dances,
a mother sings,
and a father cries.

We Are One in Divine Love. As I imagine,

I breathe and breathe and breathe.

The moon is blue. The clouds are purple.
I am but a star joining all the other stars
glistening and sparkling as we re-member our
connection to the Uni-Verse. I breathe, and
feel and watch and listen.

Every Star is singing many songs; embraced
and nurtured by Love. We are Forever ONE in
the Creator's Earth/Heart!

OFFER YOUR HAND

Offer your hand

With gratitude and patience,
I take a moment and Breathe Four Times.

I release old disappointment and
mis-understandings as lessons learned.

I Breathe.

Today I will listen and offer my good self with
kindness, and compassion.

I Breathe in Gratitude and decide to offer
my hands, my heart and my resources with a
smile!

WARM THOUGHTS

I Breathe Deeply and Thank The Master
Creator for a Joyful Awakening.

There is no doubt that it is cold and windy
with confusion outside, but in my heart the
sun is shining and beaming rays of Love.

I Breathe Deeply Six Times.
In Joyful Awakening
and Out Love!

I am a being of Love that Loves Myself and
cares enough to show Love to All Others.

Today, I have dressed for the weather of
confusion.

I Breathe and focus on warm thoughts of
Gratitude for the New Day.

I Breathe and Breathe.
In, Joyful Awakening
and
Out, Love!

EVERY BREATH
I TAKE

Every Breath I take in Gratitude clears the
pathway of hope and allows new energy to
move through me as the Breath of Love.

I listen deeply and Breathe.

In, Gratitude and
Out, Love with Compassion.

Six Times I Breathe.

In, Gratitude and
Out, Love with Compassion.

Every Breath I take in Gratitude clears the
pathway of hope and allows new energy to
move through me as the Breath of Love.

POWER OF THE SMILE

Across the Earth, every Wise Seeker Dreamer learns and appreciates the power of a smile.

A tender smile opens countless hearts and becomes an Overture to a song and dance in the beautiful Symphony of Life.

Breathe Deeply Six Times.
With each breath,

Breathe In, Appreciation.

Breathe Out, Joy.

Today, try to see the hidden good in All before you.

Open your heart for the dance.

As an Overture, offer a tender smile of appreciation, joy and gratitude!

Remember to Breathe In Appreciation and Breathe Out Joy!

BREATHE & SMILE

Beloveds, Everybody loses when you hide your gifts.

What is your gift?

How do you use your gift?

How does developing and sharing your gift benefit your community and the World?

    Breath Deeply Four Times.

How will you share your gift today?

    Breath Deeply Four Times again.

Now Smile with Confidence and say I am Grateful and Willing to Share My Gifts!

Throughout the Day, remember to Breathe and notice the beauty of the moment as you share Your Gifts!

Be a Winner!

Breathe and Smile!

BREATHE & BELIEVE

Breathe and Believe!

Patience, Kindness, Goodness and
Gentleness came for dinner and decided
to stay as permanent guests in the home
of my heart.

They brought with them Laughter, Joy,
Abiding Love, and Faith.

Together, We Breathe and Believe!

All challenges can be resolved in a good
way when you stop, think, Breathe and
Believe!

Breathe and Believe!

Breathe & Give Thanks

I Breathe Deeply and Give Thanks.

I listen and pay attention to the rhythm of my heart.

Abundant Good resides there.

I Breathe Deeply In Love.

I honor the many blessings of my life and know that Courage, Patience and Persistence travel with me.

I Breathe Deeply.

In every situation I ask for clarity so that I can offer the Abundant Good that lives in my heart.

I Say Thank You for Every Lesson, Opportunity and Blessing Shared!

I Breathe, and Step Gently Into the New Day!

Rediscovering Joy

Joy is the Transformative Healing Agent
for the Soul, Mind, Heart and Spirit!

Contagious Joy

The tender smile that you offer to yourself, and others is like a flower blossoming in the Garden of Hearts.

Your laughter is like the Holy Bell of Joy ringing through the ethers with hope; traveling across oceans, mountains, valleys and cities through the Breath of the Wind.

Your smiles and laughter are like a catalyst that awakens the leaf on every tree of life and causes them to offer oxygen of joy so that we breathe in love and harmony. Today offer your tender smiles and laughter.

Breathe Deeply, in Love
and you will become like a flower;
helping to heal many hearts!

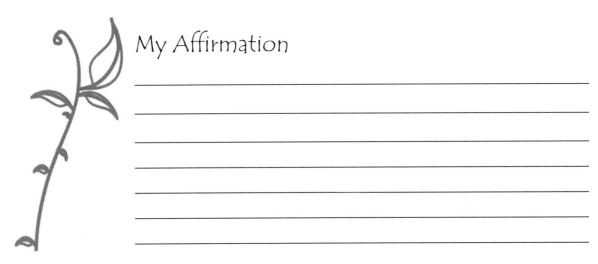

My Affirmation

_____

_____

_____

_____

_____

_____

_____

My Reflections

Amazing, Brilliant, Compassionate YOU!

Time

Time will remind us that this moment, this hour nor this day Will Come Again!

Make the most of time in your relationships. Dreamers be present in love! Smile, laugh and enjoy each other.

Be fully present in love, and as time passes, this day will become a cherished memory in your heart!

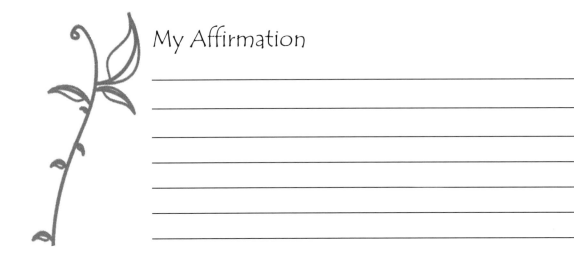

My Affirmation

_____
_____
_____
_____
_____
_____

My Reflections

_____

_____

_____

_____

_____

_____

_____

_____

_____

_____

_____

_____

_____

_____

_____

_____

_____

_____

_____

_____

_____

_____

_____

_____

_____

_____

_____

_____

_____

Amazing, Brilliant, Compassionate YOU!

Good Humor

Good Humor has come to help build new bridges and opens doors.

Now, ask Valour to help you to restore your friendship with Strength so that you learn to focus on your many gifts.

The Seeker Dreamer opens their mind and learns to become a responsible builder of bridges, nurturer of dreams and lover of heart wisdom!

Laugh and say Thank You!

My Affirmation

_____

_____

_____

_____

_____

_____

My Reflections

_____

_____

_____

_____

_____

_____

_____

_____

_____

_____

_____

_____

_____

_____

_____

_____

_____

_____

_____

_____

_____

_____

_____

_____

_____

_____

_____

_____

_____

Amazing, Brilliant, Compassionate YOU!

Let Your Joy Shine

This is a spectacular day to remember that you are a splendid human being shining from the inside out.

Feel the hope that pours through you as the breath of peace. Help make the world better!

Offer your light with humility and joy. Say hello to Grace. She will show you your next good step. Smile and Shine Dreamer.

Share the Gift of You
Shine from the inside out!

My Affirmation

_____

_____

_____

_____

_____

_____

_____

My Reflections

_____

_____

_____

_____

_____

_____

_____

_____

_____

_____

_____

_____

_____

_____

_____

_____

_____

_____

_____

_____

_____

_____

_____

_____

_____

_____

_____

_____

_____

_____

_____

_____

Amazing, Brilliant, Compassionate YOU!

Joy Oasis

When we awaken and say thank you for the miracle of the new day, we are remembering and honoring Grace by drinking from the joy oasis.

Each thank you we offer in pure gratitude comes from our joy oasis.

What is the Joy Oasis?

It is the place in our hearts where good, hope and love reside.

Drink often from your joy oasis and simple miracles will become more evident in your day.

My Affirmation

_____

_____

_____

_____

_____

_____

My Reflections

Amazing, Brilliant, Compassionate YOU!

Joy Bearer

Dreamer, now that you have awakened into the new day and offered thanks, walk with a prayer of joy.

Today use and share your gifts with humility.

Smile when you say hello!

Offer to help someone in need.

Listen carefully.

Complete each task willingly--- with precision and grace.

Share your best with joyful gratitude.
Become a Joy Bearer!

My Affirmation

_____
_____
_____
_____
_____
_____

My Reflections

Amazing, Brilliant, Compassionate YOU!

Joyful Giver

A Dreamer learns to offer each gift loving without any expectation! Be grateful that you are able to share.

Thank our Blessed Creator for allowing you to be in service to Love.

Be a Joyful Giver!

A Dreamer learns that every gift given
with genuine appreciation and hope offers
encouragement to others.

Every gift given in love multiplies in love and can bring a better destiny to both the giver and many receivers!

My Affirmation

_____

_____

_____

_____

_____

_____

My Reflections

_____

_____

_____

_____

_____

_____

_____

_____

_____

_____

_____

_____

_____

_____

_____

_____

_____

_____

_____

_____

_____

_____

_____

_____

_____

_____

_____

_____

_____

_____

_____

Amazing, Brilliant, Compassionate YOU!

Inspiration for Joy

A dreamer comes to believe that each day we awaken is a day to be thankful. Every day is a day created for gratitude and celebration!

Today, let go of past regret.

Embrace this day with joy,
hope and illuminating faith.

Life is a celebration of wonder on the journey of your dreams.

A dreamer works hard but finds time to enjoy, love and cherish the special moments with **Divine Inspiration!**

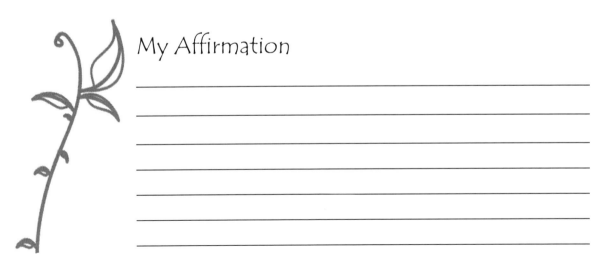

My Affirmation

_____

_____

_____

_____

_____

_____

My Reflections

Amazing, Brilliant, Compassionate YOU!

Heart Garden

Every smile, tender word or small act of kindness brings hope, nurtures and helps the seed of love blossom in our hearts, the hearts of others and the Universal Heart.

A dreamer finds tremendous joy in nurturing the gardens of our hearts!

My Affirmation

_____

_____

_____

_____

_____

_____

My Reflections

Amazing, Brilliant, Compassionate YOU!

Gratitude

Gratitude *is* the Key to Opening Your Heart and
Unlocking the Doors to Receive Widsom and Expressing Creativity!

Amazing, Brilliant, Compassionate YOU!

Gratitude

I Breathe Deeply with Gratitude.

Six Times I Breathe.
With each deep breath,
I become more Attentive
and Receptive to yielding.

I Breathe Deeply Four Times.
Only through my willingness
to yield can I honor
and move forward
with Good Change.

Today, I will be Attentive and Receptive!

I will express Gratitude!

My Affirmation

_____

_____

_____

_____

_____

_____

_____

My Reflections

Amazing, Brilliant, Compassionate YOU!

When Gratitude Came to Dinner

When Gratitude came to dinner, she brought Patience, Hope, and Mercy.

They greeted the other guests and the house filled with joy and conversation. The dreamer had invited a cousin named Confusion.

Compassion arrived just in time and sat right next to Confusion. Feeling welcomed, Confusion became calm.

Then came the Dinner Prayer of Thanks that everyone shared!

Love spoke; filling the home and hearts of every guest!

My Affirmation

_____

_____

_____

_____

_____

_____

_____

My Reflections

_____

_____

_____

_____

_____

_____

_____

_____

_____

_____

_____

_____

_____

_____

_____

_____

_____

_____

_____

_____

_____

_____

_____

_____

_____

_____

_____

_____

_____

_____

Amazing, Brilliant, Compassionate YOU!

Remembering to be Grateful

Even as a young Spirit in Heaven, I frolicked through buttercup and marigold meadows, danced with butterflies and swam with dolphins friends in the Ocean of Love.

I learned what All Dreamers learn!

I learned to be grateful for everything and everyone; and to appreciate the goodness of the CREATOR'S Agents of LOVE everywhere in the Heavens, on Earth and within the Heart!

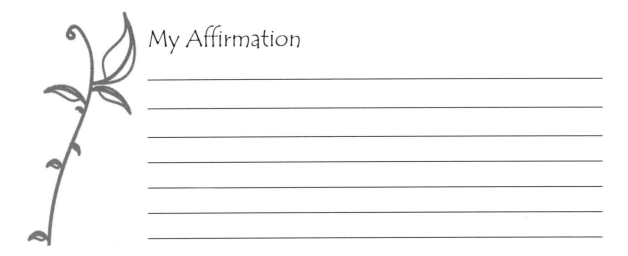

My Affirmation

_____

_____

_____

_____

_____

_____

_____

My Reflections

Amazing, Brilliant, Compassionate YOU!

Happy to be Alive

Happy to Be Alive, I begin the day with new eyes of compassion and a heart of humility.

I Breathe Deeply and clear my mind and my heart.

> *I Breathe.*
> *In, Compassion with JOY,*
> *Out, Love with Humility and Strength.*

> *Six Times with Gratitude I Breathe.*
> *In, Compassion with JOY,*
> *Out, Love with Humility and Strength.*

I become energized by Love and am filled with new Courage.

Breathing In Compassion with JOY,
Exhaling Out Love with Humility and Strength.

> *Happy to Be Alive, I Breathe!*

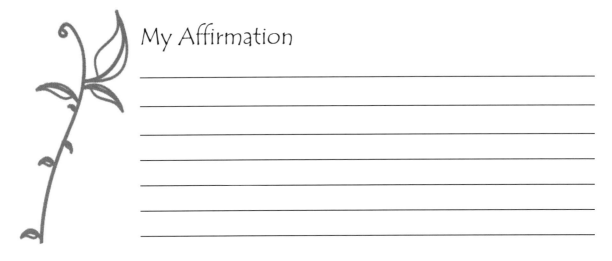

My Affirmation

_____

_____

_____

_____

_____

_____

My Reflections

Amazing, Brilliant, Compassionate YOU!

Autumn Celebration

One day the dreamer awakened with only prayers of gratitude and appreciation. Outside the air was crisp and the sun sang with understanding.

The wind whispered to begin harvesting the precious fruit of love.

Buckeyes of joy and pine cones of fresh clarity lay on fallen leaves shimmering in gold and orange became like a blanket of hope.

The dreamer sang in delight and collected autumn's gifts to share!

My Affirmation

_____

_____

_____

_____

_____

_____

_____

My Reflections

Amazing, Brilliant, Compassionate YOU!

Patient Wisdom

The one with gratitude, who lives with wisdom and love in their heart, has nothing to fear because every outcome can be accepted and managed through Patient Wisdom and Love.

I Breathe Deeply Six Times

Today I offer Gratitude for my life and Our World with Hope for Healing.

May every experience help me grow with Patient Wisdom and Love.

My Affirmation

_____

_____

_____

_____

_____

_____

_____

My Reflections

_____

_____

_____

_____

_____

_____

_____

_____

_____

_____

_____

_____

_____

_____

_____

_____

_____

_____

_____

_____

_____

_____

_____

_____

_____

_____

_____

_____

_____

_____

Amazing, Brilliant, Compassionate YOU!

I Bend In Gratitude!

In stormy weather, a pilot will tell you that in order to get to your good destination, it is always necessary to fly above or around the storm.

I Breathe Deeply and ask myself, *"What would it take for me to travel around the every obstacle with a hopeful heart?"*. The answer is clear:

First, I must have Gratitude for every lesson.
Second, I must have patience.
Third, I must learn to be flexible and bend like a
        Willow Tree in Love with the Earth.

I Breathe Deeply.
       In, Patience, Out, Flexibility with Love.
Ten times I Breathe.
       In, Patience, Out, Flexibility with Love.
Today I am patient and flexible.

Like a Willow Tree in Love with the Earth, I bend in Gratitude and Respect!

My Affirmation

_____

_____

_____

_____

_____

_____

_____

My Reflections

_____
_____
_____
_____
_____
_____
_____
_____
_____
_____
_____
_____
_____
_____
_____
_____
_____
_____
_____
_____
_____
_____
_____
_____
_____
_____
_____
_____
_____
_____
_____
_____

Amazing, Brilliant, Compassionate YOU!

Thank You is My Prayer Today

Thank You!

I Breathe Deeply Seven Times.
In, Hope and Mercy, and Out, Patience and Love.

Through every moment of conflict and confusion,
I ground my thoughts and my heart in peace.

Listening, I Breathe and Breathe.
In, Hope and Mercy, and
Out, Patience and Love.

With JOY I Breathe, Listen and Say Thank YOU!

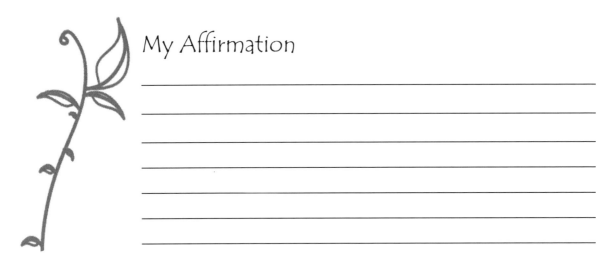

My Affirmation

_____

_____

_____

_____

_____

_____

_____

My Reflections

_____

_____

_____

_____

_____

_____

_____

_____

_____

_____

_____

_____

_____

_____

_____

_____

_____

_____

_____

_____

_____

_____

_____

_____

_____

_____

_____

_____

_____

Amazing, Brilliant, Compassionate YOU!

Profound Gratitude

Our friends offer us the gifts of compassion and kindness.

They reflect love unselfishly and honor our journeys. Friends offer honesty, are truthful and learn to love us just as we are!

They laugh with us, cry with us and share our hopes and dreams.

A friend will lovingly do for you what you can't do for your self and help you rise to every occasion!

Today, dreamer offer your profound gratitude to a friend!

My Affirmation

_____

_____

_____

_____

_____

_____

_____

My Reflections

Amazing, Brilliant, Compassionate YOU!

Dreaming Faith and Hope

The Birds are singing with Joy.
The Sun is shining with Hope.
Clouds of Faith linger with Compassion and Understanding.
It is truly a Glorious New Day!

> I Breathe In the Oxygen of Love.
> I Breathe Out the Newness of Love's Restorative Power.
>
> Eight Times I Breathe Deeply.
> With each breath I am filled with appreciation and Love.
>
> I Breathe Deeply.

I offer my Gratitude for the miraculous gift of Life. With Humility, Joy, Patience and Respect for Others ... I Step into the Mystery of the Glorious New Day!

Faith

A dreamer may fall or lose their way in material bliss, but when they remember the Creator's good dream for their life —

With Faith and Hope, they will rise with renewed vigor and strength filled with the hope needed to take the next step into their good destiny.

Faith is the tool every dreamer needs
to honor and
lovingly live their divine purpose!

My Affirmation

_____

_____

_____

_____

_____

_____

My Reflections

Amazing, Brilliant, Compassionate YOU!

Swish, Swish, Ting!

On this day everything seemed to go wrong and the dreamer cried. There was a sound far in the distance.

> "Swish, swish, ting! Ting, ting!".

Then the sound came closer and began to vibrate all around and moved right into the dreamer's heart.

> "Swish, swish, ting! Ting, ting!
> Swish, swish, ting! Ting, ting!"

The dreamer's tears paved the way for a new idea. In the Spirit Realm, angels danced in celebration as Hope, Possibility, and Faith left to assist the dreamer!

> "Swish, swish, ting! Ting, ting!"

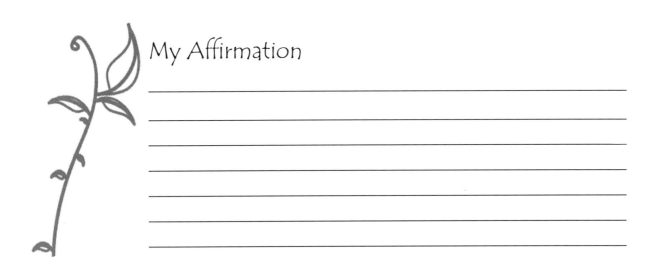

My Affirmation

_____

_____

_____

_____

_____

_____

_____

My Reflections

_____

_____

_____

_____

_____

_____

_____

_____

_____

_____

_____

_____

_____

_____

_____

_____

_____

_____

_____

_____

_____

_____

_____

_____

_____

_____

_____

_____

Amazing, Brilliant, Compassionate YOU!

Loves Reward

On this day, the MasterMotherFatherCreator smiled and the sun glistened through the clouds of greed, selfishness and mis-understanding.

Across the Earth-Heart, many dreamers awakened with re-newed hope and wanted to honor all that was good.

They offered gratitude for their lives and asked for Mercy and Courage to come into their hearts.

Love smiled and as a reward sent Patience, Respect and Faith!

My Affirmation

_____

_____

_____

_____

_____

_____

_____

My Reflections

_____
_____
_____
_____
_____
_____
_____
_____
_____
_____
_____
_____
_____
_____
_____
_____
_____
_____
_____
_____
_____
_____
_____
_____
_____
_____
_____
_____

Amazing, Brilliant, Compassionate YOU!

A Universal Melody

In life, discord is inevitable, but a dreamer often discovers and develops a unique voice of caring, compassion and joy through play, practice and hard work!

When you have the desire and fortitude to embrace the rhythm of your heart, then you will sing your lovesong and the harmony of your life will attune itself to the Universal Melody!

My Affirmation

_____

_____

_____

_____

_____

_____

_____

My Reflections

Amazing, Brilliant, Compassionate YOU!

Capable You

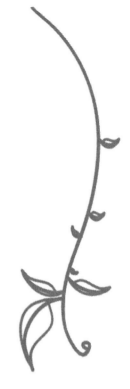

Everything you have ever done has prepared you for this moment.

Embrace this day of Grace with appreciation. Honor All Divine Creations.

Through your visions of good, you, dreamer are now prepared and destined to re-new your life purpose.

Give thanks for the gift of Hope's allegiance.
Give thanks for the friendship of Faith.
Give thanks to our Blessed Creator.

Walk in gratitude and you will feel yourself shift into a more Confident, Capable, Compassionate Loving You!

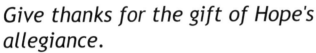

My Affirmation

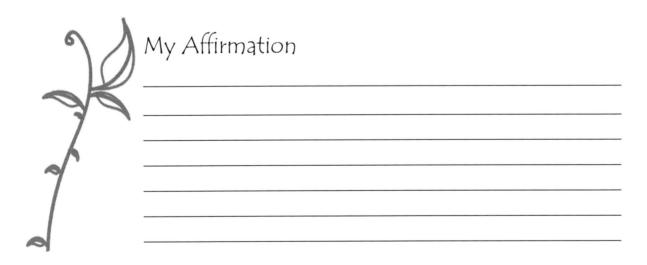

_____

_____

_____

_____

_____

_____

_____

My Reflections

Amazing, Brilliant, Compassionate YOU!

Today Offers New Opportunity

The Dreamer knew he had failed and still he sang with Gratitude and Joy.

He knew that though he had made mistakes, he learned to love himself was still worthy of sharing and receiving love.

As he gave thanks, Mercy filled his heart with understanding. Yesterday had offered an important lesson.

Today Always Offers New Opportunity!

My Affirmation

_____

_____

_____

_____

_____

_____

_____

My Reflections

Amazing, Brilliant, Compassionate YOU!

Captain Willingness

The Angel Dreamer prayed for guidance as she boarded the Hope Ship with Courage.

The destination was Earth.

At dinner, the Angel Dreamer met Charity who was traveling with Understanding, Forgiveness and Compassion.

Enthusiasm was there with Encouragement and Joy. Faith came late and brought Acceptance.

In celebration, Captain Willingness invited them all to the dance floor as Mystery and Love Sang a Song of Grace!

My Affirmation

_____

_____

_____

_____

_____

_____

_____

My Reflections

_____

_____

_____

_____

_____

_____

_____

_____

_____

_____

_____

_____

_____

_____

_____

_____

_____

_____

_____

_____

_____

_____

_____

_____

_____

_____

_____

_____

Amazing, Brilliant, Compassionate YOU!

One Step Forward

When I lost myself in the dream of disappointment,
Deep Sorrow greeted me in tears.

He spoke of the battles and wars we had created in
fear and self- judgment.

> "This pain and vulnerability you feel is an opening
> for Faith. You are a Seeker Dreamer. Choose to
> Move On!"

And then he was gone. I awakened and saw my
friends, Mercy and Forgiveness. *"Come,"* they said,

> "Healing begins with One Step Forward
> into Yourself on the Pathway of Love!"

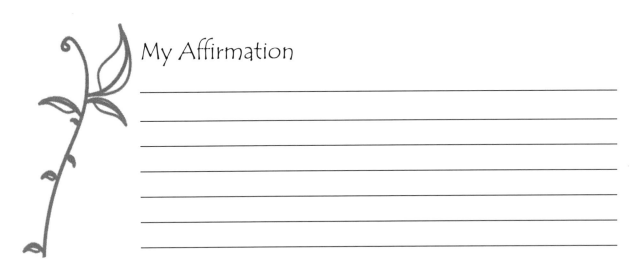

My Affirmation

_____

_____

_____

_____

_____

_____

My Reflections

_____

_____

_____

_____

_____

_____

_____

_____

_____

_____

_____

_____

_____

_____

_____

_____

_____

_____

_____

_____

_____

_____

_____

_____

_____

_____

_____

_____

_____

_____

_____

Amazing, Brilliant, Compassionate YOU!

Be A Witness

Every Seeker Dreamer Will Journey.

They may never leave the town they were born; yet, they will climb mountains of fear and triumph in a valley of hope.

They will cross barren deserts of despair and find an oasis of understanding.

They will swim through lakes of joy and sail the ocean of wisdom.

All this the Seeker Dreamer does as they witness, learn, change, grow and become their true self in Love!

My Affirmation

_____

_____

_____

_____

_____

_____

_____

My Reflections

Amazing, Brilliant, Compassionate YOU!

Praticing Patience

Prune With Patience!

You will never know how the Creator meant for you to blossom if you are not willing to dig deep into the dirt of the Earth. Till your heart's soil with delight. Learn from the weeds of disappointment. Create a strong, healthy foundation. Plant new dream seeds with hope. Prune with patience. Celebrate every bud and honor the roots with care.

Share your flowers when they bloom and blossom.

Amazing, Brilliant, Compassionate YOU!

Patience and Tenacity

In every life negotiation, we must be both receptive and resourceful.

Our ego must give way to objective reasoning and perceptive vision.

Patience and Tenacity aid us as we face obstacles with gracious understanding.

A Seeker Dreamer becomes more resourceful and receptive to new opportunities when they listen deeply, adjust communication and honor the new possibility that clear vision brings through Divine Grace.

My Affirmation

_____

_____

_____

_____

_____

_____

My Reflections

_____

_____

_____

_____

_____

_____

_____

_____

_____

_____

_____

_____

_____

_____

_____

_____

_____

_____

_____

_____

_____

_____

_____

_____

_____

_____

_____

_____

_____

Amazing, Brilliant, Compassionate YOU!

Harvest of Love

Every dreamer learns that a garden does not blossom overnight. It may take a lifetime.

Patience guides the dreamer through the seasons of life as she teaches compassion and the courage to nurture and love the garden even when there is no fruit.

There may be freezing winters, frosty, cold springs and hot, hot summers.

Many seasons may pass, but because you still believe and teach your children to believe ... one day, the harvest of Love will come and feed the whole world community!

My Affirmation

_____

_____

_____

_____

_____

_____

_____

My Reflections

_____
_____
_____
_____
_____
_____
_____
_____
_____
_____
_____
_____
_____
_____
_____
_____
_____
_____
_____
_____
_____
_____
_____
_____
_____
_____
_____
_____
_____
_____

Amazing, Brilliant, Compassionate YOU!

The Greatest Lie

The greatest lie we tell ourselves is that good change is not possible!

A dreamer who awakens in love will meet many obstacles and be told that there is no hope for good change.

Disappointment will become his shadow.
Still, Faith will guide him.
Wisdom will protect him.

Years will pass but the dreamer's good efforts will continue. Children will watch and listen to the dreamer. **They will not believe the lie**.

Children will learn and share with joy and one day, the floodgate of good change will come!

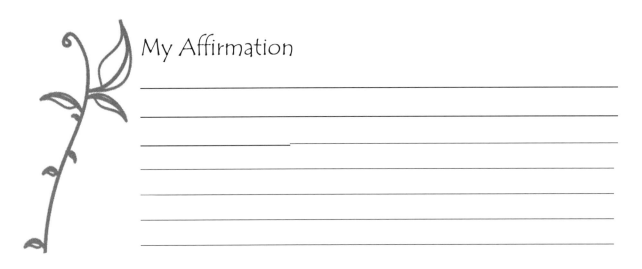

My Affirmation

_____

_____

_____   _____

_____

_____

_____

_____

My Reflections

Amazing, Brilliant, Compassionate YOU!

The Wisdom Trail

All days are good days when a dreamer awakens in gratitude! Some days are difficult.

A dreamer accepts difficulty as a lesson and realizes that there is great strength in learning humility.

The wisdom trail will reveal our weakness and help us grow in flexibility.

Even in difficulty, the dreamer offers gratitude; practices compassion; becomes more flexible and embraces the wisdom and lessons of love!

My Affirmation

_____

_____

_____

_____

_____

_____

_____

My Reflections

Amazing, Brilliant, Compassionate YOU!

Honor the New Season

How must you change so that you honor the New Season?

Nothing you have done has been in vain. Look at what you've already accomplished. You have laid a strong foundation. Now, prepare for the New Season. The soil is fertile.

What good dream seeds have you planted
with Hope and Faith?

Every day say Thank You. Try to offer kindness to All.   You are preparing for A New Season!

Your Dream will surely take time to blossom!
Just Continue to Work Hard and Nurture the Garden of Your Heart!

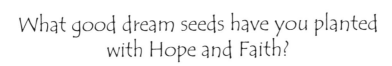

My Affirmation

_____

_____

_____

_____

_____

_____

My Reflections

Amazing, Brilliant, Compassionate YOU!

I Offer This Day

I Offer This Day in Contemplation.

Breathing Deeply Eight Times, I allow Gratitude to pour through my heart.

I Breathe In Gratitude with Patience.
I Exhale with an Openness to Listen and Receive.

I accept every opportunity to re-visit ways that I can better communicate; as well as to pay attention to the signs and details asking me to step forward.

I Offer This Day in Contemplation. I will listen, be patience and watchful!

Four Times I Breathe In Gratitude with Patience.

With Each Breath, I Exhale with an Openness to Listen and Receive.

I Breathe With Gratitude and Patience.

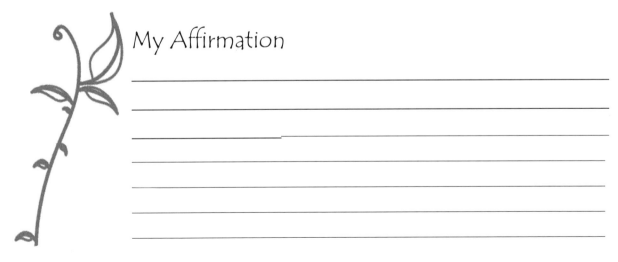

My Affirmation

_____

_____

_____

_____

_____

_____

_____

My Reflections

Amazing, Brilliant, Compassionate YOU!

If You Believe

The Wise One said to the Seeker…

"All is possible only if you believe!"

Try to awaken with peace in your heart.

Breathe Deeply Four Times
and say Thank You.

Decide to take one step into good change with
Joy! Always remember to work and offer your
best throughout the day.

Breathe Deeply Four Times
and say Thank You.

Today take a Step into the Good Change You
Believe Is Possible and Probable!"

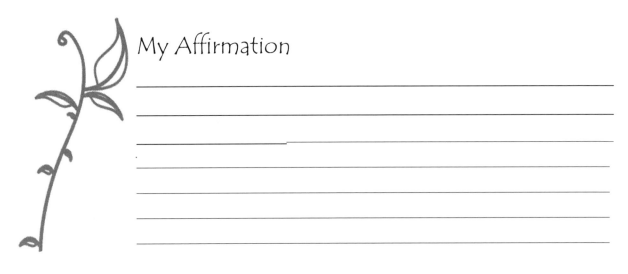

My Affirmation

_____

_____

_____   _____

_____

_____

_____

_____

My Reflections

Amazing, Brilliant, Compassionate YOU!

Breathe With Patience

I Begin this day breathing with patience believing that I am a being of Love born with the gifts of Kindness and Respect.

These gifts, Kindness and Respect join with Patience and daily nurture me.

I Breathe Deeply Six Times.

> In, Gratitude and Kindness.
> Out, Respect with Patience and Love.

Every breath is born of Love.

> In, Gratitude and Kindness.
> Out, Respect with Patience and Love.

I Breathe Deeply and remember...

> With Patience I am able to offer the gifts of Respect and Kindness to All!

My Affirmation

_____

_____

_____

_____

_____

_____

My Reflections

_____

_____

_____

_____

_____

_____

_____

_____

_____

_____

_____

_____

_____

_____

_____

_____

_____

_____

_____

_____

_____

_____

_____

_____

_____

_____

_____

Amazing, Brilliant, Compassionate YOU!

New Beginnings

Change is a constant in our lives.

A dreamer who experiences the loss of a job, a home, a family member or dear friend learns to mourn and then let go of the familiar.

By honoring all the good memories within our hearts, every dreamer learns to accept and embrace the gift of a wondrous New Beginning.

More good awaits the dreamer
on the Road of Love!

My Affirmation

_____

_____

_____   _____

_____

_____

_____

_____

My Reflections

Amazing, Brilliant, Compassionate YOU!

Releasing Limitations

I make a promise to myself.

I will learn to swim the rivers and oceans of unknowing.

I will climb the mountains of hope and walk across deserts of new understanding.

I will rest on beaches and reflect in the valleys.

I will allow the oasis of my heart to become renewed through my consistent discipline and good efforts to grow.

Still Your Mind and Listen to Your Heart

Now, Breathe.
In, Worthiness and Out, Capability.
Breathe Deeply Six Times.
In, Worthiness and Out, Capability.

First of all, acknowledge that you are a worthy, capable individual. Be consistent and disciplined in your efforts as you plant new seeds and lay the groundwork for growth and opportunity.

Share your harvest and build good relationships.

Be flexible and patient as you grow and change.

Breathe.
In Worthiness and Out Capability.

Risk will be required. Start Today Dreamer.
You Are Worthy and Capable of Good Fortune!

My Affirmation

_____

_____

_____

_____

_____

_____

_____

My Reflections

Amazing, Brilliant, Compassionate YOU!

In Difficulty

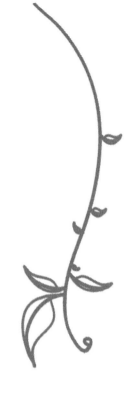

Many in great difficulty have heard the reassuring voice that says,

"I will walk with you throughout life.
Sometimes it will appear that I am behind you.
Other times that I am ahead or beside you.
When you fall I will pick you up.

Have faith and believe.
Like a phoenix, we will fly with hope
and share Our Love."

When we listen to the VOICE, we embrace peace and understand that the Infinite Power of Love resides within each of us!

We Are Never Alone!

My Affirmation

_____

_____

_____

_____

_____

_____

_____

My Reflections

_____
_____
_____
_____
_____
_____
_____
_____
_____
_____
_____
_____
_____
_____
_____
_____
_____
_____
_____
_____
_____
_____
_____
_____
_____
_____
_____
_____

Amazing, Brilliant, Compassionate YOU!

Many Questions, No Answers!

As a Dreamer you may have to give up the comfort of the safe life you've always known.

There will be many questions, and no answers.

It may feel that with each step you take, you have journeyed far from the world you knew.

Feeling alone, kindness may come from strangers.

You will meet Bravery. Deep listening and Intuition will be your guides. Patience and Faith will lovingly sing the songs of support you need!

My Affirmation

_____

_____

_____

_____

_____

_____

_____

My Reflections

_____

_____

_____

_____

_____

_____

_____

_____

_____

_____

_____

_____

_____

_____

_____

_____

_____

_____

_____

_____

_____

_____

_____

_____

_____

_____

_____

_____

_____

Amazing, Brilliant, Compassionate YOU!

Prism of Hope

Life was difficult with war and suffering. The people prayed. Some walked believing that Good could prevail.

G-d answered with a Song.

Across the planet, the Song brought the Sun. People's Smiles became like Rainbows after generations of stormy rains.

In the Sun, dreamers hearts glistened with vibrant colors and of respect.

Dreamers saw each other through the Prism of Hope and became Bright Lights singing of Love!

My Affirmation

_____

_____

_____

_____

_____

_____

My Reflections

_____

_____

_____

_____

_____

_____

_____

_____

_____

_____

_____

_____

_____

_____

_____

_____

_____

_____

_____

_____

_____

_____

_____

_____

_____

_____

_____

Amazing, Brilliant, Compassionate YOU!

Releasing Limitations of Fear

One day, the dreamer became a dolphin and with Commitment swam into the depth of the ocean of her inner-self to meet her friend Clarity.

The deeper she swam,
the less fearful she became.

She learned to Breathe Love and her heart opened with guidance from Courage and his friend Compassion.

Traveling back to the surface, the dreamer became human again but she was never alone.

Every time she Breathed Love, the dreamer re-membered that Commitment, Clarity, Courage and Compassion were Living In Her Heart!

My Affirmation

_____

_____

_____

_____

_____

_____

_____

My Reflections

Amazing, Brilliant, Compassionate YOU!

Not Enough

Love that is equal and special, begins when you honor the Creator's Gifts in You.

You choose abundance and joy as you use your gifts and learn resilient communication.

Let go of Not Enough!

Today Dreamer, All that You Need — You Have.

Give Thanks!

With this New Day comes a more flexible, prosperous New You in partnership with the Creator!

Give Thanks!

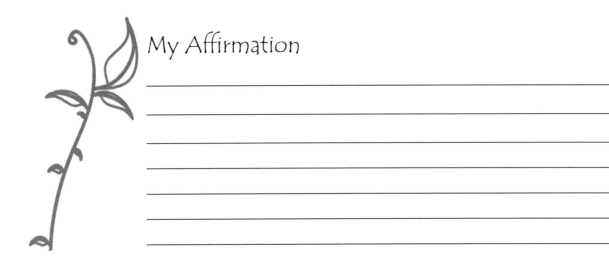

My Affirmation

_____

_____

_____

_____

_____

_____

My Reflections

Amazing, Brilliant, Compassionate YOU!

Deep Regret

It was only in the Autumn of Life, that the Master Dreamer was able to meet Deep Regret in the Garden of Yesterday's Sorrow.

Like old lovers, they sat together, held hands under the Tree of Life; drank ginger tea mixed with tears and the sweet honey of forgiveness.

And that night in a dream: the twins — Joy and Reconciliation were conceived and Re-Born in Love!

My Affirmation

_____

_____

_____

_____

_____

_____

My Reflections

Amazing, Brilliant, Compassionate YOU!

Deep Confusion

When there is deep confusion in our hearts, before moving forward we must rest, and wait for Clarity.

Every Seeker Dreamer may journey and discover a river of Doubt. Don't dive in or you may drown in negativity.

Rest your mind, your body and your heart.

Wait until daylight.

The Ferry of Truth and Understanding is on the way to take you across to your next Good Destination.

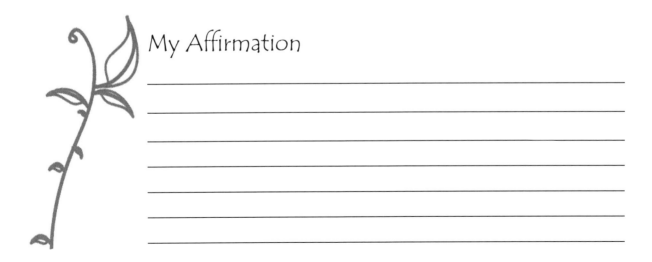

My Affirmation

_____

_____

_____

_____

_____

_____

My Reflections

Amazing, Brilliant, Compassionate YOU!

Turtle Believer

Like the Turtle Believer, every Seeker Dreamer must learn to be objective and pursue a balanced path.

When a Scorpion asks for a lift, the Turtle Believer smiles and wishes him well but continues to travel into the water alone.

If you are a Turtle Believer, who is the Scorpion to whom you must bid farewell so that you are able to freely swim into the Waters of Your Good Destiny?

My Affirmation

_____

_____

_____

_____

_____

_____

_____

My Reflections

Amazing, Brilliant, Compassionate YOU!

Compassion and Kindness

A Smile can share joy, give
hope
or offer compassion.

Amazing, Brilliant, Compassionate YOU!

Make Kindness Your Mantra

Even when there are no words, there is still communication.

Listen in the silence and feel the connection to All around you!

A dreamer learns to feel the heart of the Uni-Verse as they accept our Creator's Grace.

Today, breathe deeply
Make kindness your mantra.

Commit to walk as a being of Loving Grace!

My Affirmation

_____

_____

_____

_____

_____

_____

My Reflections

_____

_____

_____

_____

_____

_____

_____

_____

_____

_____

_____

_____

_____

_____

_____

_____

_____

_____

_____

_____

_____

_____

_____

_____

_____

_____

_____

_____

Amazing, Brilliant, Compassionate YOU!

Seeds of Good

I imagine that All before me have within them
the seeds of good.

I will continue to nurture the garden of
humanity with smiles, good wishes and dreams
of peace.

Even when another is stubborn, I offer my
cooperation with compassionate care and honor
our collective values.

My Affirmation

_____

_____

_____

_____

_____

_____

My Reflections

Amazing, Brilliant, Compassionate YOU!

The Quiet Dreamer

Many are quiet dreamers.

They listen and feel intently.

They may say little with words but their actions provide good care and offer solutions.

Through their hearts we learn compassion.

Sometimes our good actions are the gift that provides comfort and healing when there are no words!

My Affirmation

_____

_____

_____

_____

_____

_____

My Reflections

_____

_____

_____

_____

_____

_____

_____

_____

_____

_____

_____

_____

_____

_____

_____

_____

_____

_____

_____

_____

_____

_____

_____

_____

_____

_____

_____

Amazing, Brilliant, Compassionate YOU!

Light Your Pathway!

Light your pathway of life with a Smile.

Every Sincere Smile is a beautiful gift.

A Smile can share joy, give hope or offer compassion.

I Breathe Deeply Six Times.
In, JOY.   Out, Compassion and Hope.
In, Joy.   Out, Compassion and Hope.

Today I will to light my pathway of life with Compassion, Hope and Joy!

I Breathe Deeply In Gratitude
and Smile!

My Affirmation

_____

_____

_____

_____

_____

_____

My Reflections

_____

_____

_____

_____

_____

_____

_____

_____

_____

_____

_____

_____

_____

_____

_____

_____

_____

_____

_____

_____

_____

_____

_____

_____

_____

_____

_____

_____

Amazing, Brilliant, Compassionate YOU!

An Overture

Across the Earth, every Wise Seeker Dreamer
learns and appreciates the power of a smile.

A tender smile opens countless hearts and
becomes an Overture to a song and dance in
the beautiful Symphony of Life.

Today, seeing the Divine in All,
open your heart for the dance.

As an Overture, offer a tender smile of
appreciation, joy and gratitude!

My Affirmation

_____

_____

_____

_____

_____

_____

My Reflections

Amazing, Brilliant, Compassionate YOU!

Saying Less

A dreamer must be mindful that their words do not harm but heal.

Even when we don't mean to offend, sometimes the very tone of our words become weapons that harm.

A dreamer learns to have more understanding, and to say less, with more compassion.

Ultimately, a dreamer's consistent good thoughts and actions will speak louder than the words!

My Affirmation

_____

_____

_____

_____

_____

_____

My Reflections

Amazing, Brilliant, Compassionate YOU!

Good Service

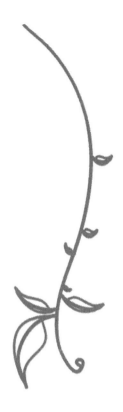

A dreamer learns that offering help with a gentle, good spirit teaches us to open our hearts and receive the gift of gratitude.

We learn to be grateful that we have the talent and resources to be of good service to others!

Today, How Can You Offer Help?

My Affirmation

_____

_____

_____

_____

_____

_____

My Reflections

Amazing, Brilliant, Compassionate YOU!

Life Circumstances

We can not presume that we always understand the intricacy or delicate nature of the life circumstances of one another.

Still, we always have the opportunity to meet each other heart to heart — even in disappointment; and, especially when they are not able to meet our needs or desire.

A Seeker Dreamer learns to forego judgment while offering loving compassion and concern for the well-being of others without expectation!

My Affirmation

_____

_____

_____

_____

_____

_____

_____

My Reflections

Amazing, Brilliant, Compassionate YOU!

Be A Friend!

Be a friend and journey through life with Love beyond expectation. Be thankful for how the Creator speaks to you through a friend. They will often be the one to support you through a health, family or personal crisis.

A friend will hold a space for you to breathe; and travel with you through the joys and sorrows of life.

A friend is a member of your spiritual family with a bond created in mutual acceptance, respect, and shared history.

Every True Friendship is Embodied By Abiding, Limitless Love.

Breathe Deeply.
In, Gratitude.
Out, Love.
Be A Friend!

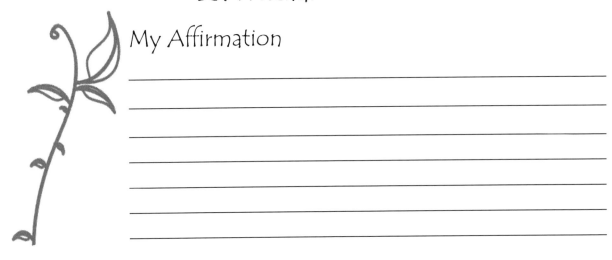

My Affirmation

_____

_____

_____

_____

_____

_____

My Reflections

Amazing, Brilliant, Compassionate YOU!

Trusting the Need
Not to Control

"We like to believe there are things we control, but the reality is there is nothing we truly control, not even our own feeble actions."

I Breathe Deeply Four Times.
Today, I let go of my need for control.

Trust

When we realize that we have been deceived, and trust has been violated, our hearts may feel wounded. *How do we move forward in Truth?*

First, we must accept the difficult lesson.

Second, we must remember that with every difficult lesson comes the opportunity for forgiveness so that we are able to heal our hearts and grow wiser with integrity.

Today, I Breathe Deeply Six Times.
With each breath I ask to be given Guidance
with Integrity.

I Breathe and Breathe.
In, Guidance with Integrity.
Out, Wisdom with Healing, Forgiveness and Love.

Every Truth allows me to grow, heal and move forward with Love.

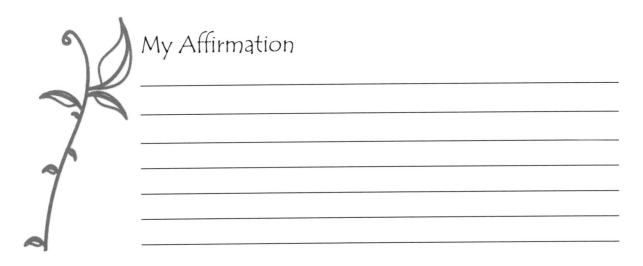

My Affirmation

_____
_____
_____
_____
_____
_____

My Reflections

Amazing, Brilliant, Compassionate YOU!

Embracing Uncertainty

Today, I let go of confusion
and embrace uncertainty.

I Breathe, and Re-Member that my every good action brings Hope.

I Breathe and allow Love to move
through my entire Be-ing.

Today, I embrace uncertainty, knowing truth will be revealed through Love.

I have unlimited patience, creativity and a commitment to have only right thoughts, words and actions.

I Breathe, and Say Thank You
for My Beautiful Life!

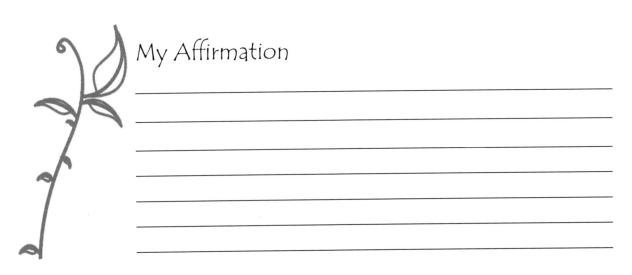

My Affirmation

_____

_____

_____

_____

_____

_____

My Reflections

Amazing, Brilliant, Compassionate YOU!

Intent

The Wise Man said to the Seeker *"We like to believe there are things we control, but the reality is there is nothing we truly control, not even our own feeble actions."*

Today, I let go of my need for control.
I Breathe Deeply Four Times.

As I learn to speak Joy and Gratitude into the Day, I will allow for each moment to flow with Divine Intent and Purpose.

I Breathe In the Joy of Aliveness.
I Breathe Out Gratitude.
Four Times I Breathe.

Giving up the idea of control, I speak Joy and Gratitude into this Day!   I will do my best to allow each moment to flow with Divine Intent and Purpose.

Two Times I Breathe!
Live With Grace

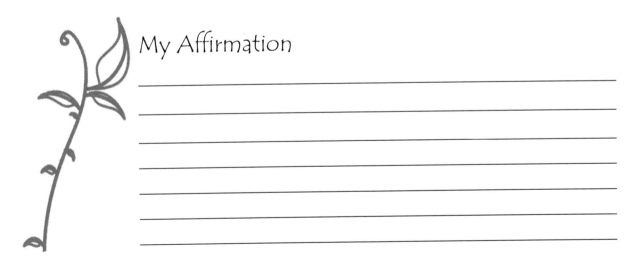

My Affirmation

_____
_____
_____
_____
_____
_____

My Reflections

Your Greatest Gifts

ALL experiences hold a lesson of new understanding about ourselves.

The Dreamer learns to pay attention to All and is inspired by both the hardships and success of others.

Every Dreamer learns that if they are to succeed in developing and fully using their gifts, they must face many obstacles.

These obstacles serve only to teach compassion, kindness and courage as one learns the power and strength of the gift of love!

My Affirmation

_____

_____

_____

_____

_____

_____

My Reflections

Amazing, Brilliant, Compassionate YOU!

New Doors

Life will ask us to let go and move on!

Sometimes it is difficult but what awaits us in love is better than our minds or egos can anticipate.

Every step we take is special. Cherish the moment.

Hone your skills of caring and compassion.

Prepare to move on with your soul's purpose.

Keep your heart open.

Follow the Divine Path of Forgiveness.

Love, hard work and patience will open New Doors of Grace!

 My Affirmation

_____

_____

_____

_____

_____

_____

My Reflections

Amazing, Brilliant, Compassionate YOU!

Learn, Receive, Share and Serve

We are born to Learn, Receive, Share and Serve.

Everyday a dreamer is learning to graciously accept the help of others and mirror their compassion and kindness in everyday actions.

I *learn* as I receive and offer a sincere thank you with a heart of gratitude.

I *share* knowing it gives me Joy.

I *serve* because it gives me Purpose!

My Affirmation

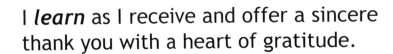

_____

_____

_____

_____

_____

_____

My Reflections

Amazing, Brilliant, Compassionate YOU!

Grow In Every Season

The Wise Man said to the Seeker,

"The cold makes me long for warmth, and warmth makes me nostalgic for the cold."

So often we half-listen with our ears and not listen to the call for the change of seasons within our hearts.

I Greet This Day with JOY and
Breathe Deeply Seven Times.

Today, I will listen deeply to my heart.

I will honor the need to grow and gently make good change throughout every season of my life!

My Affirmation

_____

_____

_____

_____

_____

_____

My Reflections

Amazing, Brilliant, Compassionate YOU!

Heed the Call

First I heed the call of Love that beckons me
to awaken into the new day.

I Breathe Deeply Six Times.
In, Gratitude for the New Day.
Out, Love with Patient Understanding.
I Breathe and feel and listen.

The Wind sings and vibrates through the air.

I Breathe.
In, Gratitude for the New Day.
Out, Love with Patient Understanding.
I Breathe and feel and listen.

I know that as I am able to offer gratitude;
so the fruit of my heart will blossom in Love.

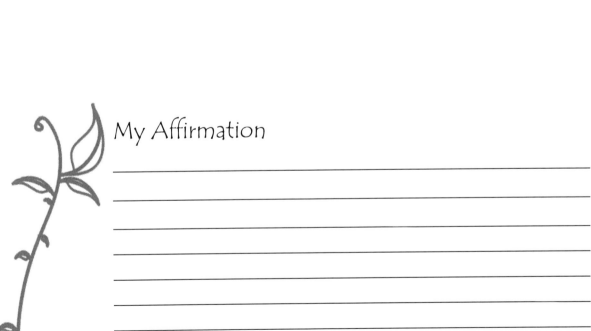

My Affirmation

_____

_____

_____

_____

_____

_____

My Reflections

_____

_____

_____

_____

_____

_____

_____

_____

_____

_____

_____

_____

_____

_____

_____

_____

_____

_____

_____

_____

_____

_____

_____

_____

_____

_____

_____

_____

Amazing, Brilliant, Compassionate YOU!

Trust

Sometimes we are quick to judge when someone acts, looks or speaks differently than us.

A Seeker Dreamer offers a hand with compassion; looks into the eyes with wisdom and sees the heart of All.

Today offer a hand.

Allow your eyes to have wisdom and compassion.

Trust that when hearts meet, Truth, whatever it is, will be revealed!

My Affirmation

_____

_____

_____

_____

_____

_____

My Reflections

Amazing, Brilliant, Compassionate YOU!

Committing to Love and Forgiveness

With clarity I commit to allow myself to be a vessel of Divine Peace so that my words and actions are able to be like the water of integrity and valour that flows, nurtures, and through Faith; brings Hope to Me, and All whose lives I touch!

Let's begin with a commitment to love and forgiveness.

Wisdom with Love

It is possible that those you have cared for, supported and loved will not stand by you when you Awaken, honor, speak and live with Integrity in Love's Truth.

Breathe Deeply Ten Times ...

Breathe
In, Understanding
Out, Wisdom with Love.

Your heart may feel like it's breaking and tears may come.

Just keep Breathing ...

In, Understanding
Out, Wisdom with Love.

 My Affirmation

_____

_____

_____

_____

_____

_____

My Reflections

Amazing, Brilliant, Compassionate YOU!

Understanding

There are people who walk with blinders.

They are caught up and intoxicated by materialism and immediate gratification. They know the price of everything. They fear losing what they have acquired and often have forgotten the value of Love.

Never Forget, You May Have Been One of Them, Yesterday.

> Breathe
> In, Understanding and
> Out, Wisdom with Love.

Be hopeful and pray for all those who have not yet awakened.

> Breathe
> In, Understanding
> Out ,Wisdom.

Love has no price tag and its value is Infinite.
Live with Integrity In Love's Truth.

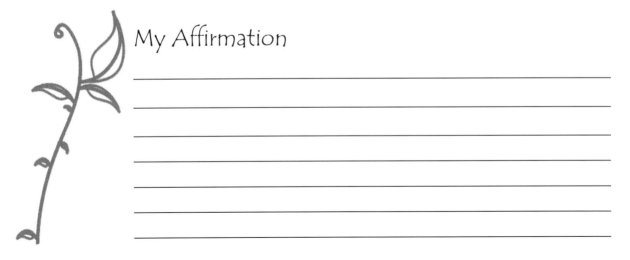

My Affirmation

_____

_____

_____

_____

_____

_____

_____

My Reflections

Amazing, Brilliant, Compassionate YOU!

Misunderstandings

Often, we have wounded each other in so many ways; we expect to be hurt and disappointed. And because we expect it, we find a reason to be hurt or disappointed. There is so much misunderstanding in the world.

Today I will see the best in myself and others. I offer only my best.

> I Breathe Deeply Four Times.
> With each breath I honor the gift of Love.

I am able to give graciously and forgive easily. I let go of every thought of disappointment.

> I Breathe In, Love
> Out, Joy with Gratitude for Every Experience!
> I Breathe.

Today, I will see the best in myself and others. I honor the gift of Love. I am able to give graciously and forgive easily.

> I move forward and remember to Breathe!
> In, Love.
> Out, Joy with Gratitude!

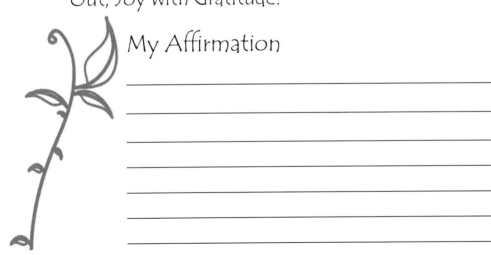

My Affirmation

_____

_____

_____

_____

_____

_____

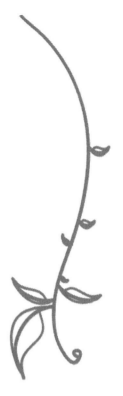

My Reflections

Amazing, Brilliant, Compassionate YOU!

May the Wealth of Our Love

I Breathe Deeply Four Times.
With each breath I honor the Creator
with my gratitude and humility.

I Breathe and offer a prayer.

May the wealth of Our Love create many
abundant hearts that multiply and share the
gifts and messages of healing, cooperative
peace and the energy of prosperity that lives in
Our Souls!

I Breathe and Breathe.
I Breathe and with Courage,
I open my heart to Believe!

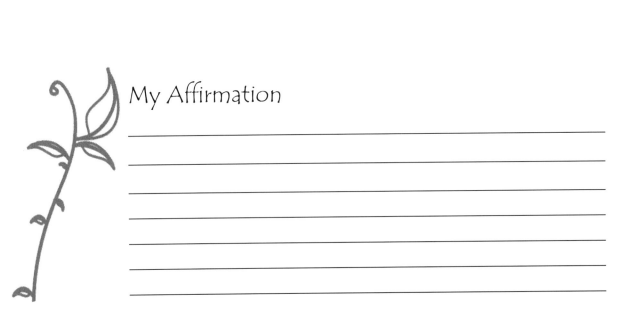

My Affirmation

_____

_____

_____

_____

_____

_____

_____

My Reflections

Amazing, Brilliant, Compassionate YOU!

Love Is Unforgettable

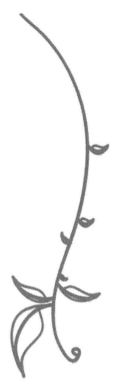

Because Love Is Unforgettable, I know that today I will need to dress myself with Courage, Compassion and Forgiveness.

I Breathe Deeply Six Times and offer Gratitude to all those I Love and have ever Loved.

Today, I have dressed myself with Courage, Compassion and Forgiveness. I will walk my talk and offer my very best with Joy.

And because Love Is Unforgettable, I will Breathe and Breathe with Loving appreciation and remember to honor all that is beautiful about my life, my loved ones and our Earth-Heart!

I Breathe Deeply with Unforgettable Love!

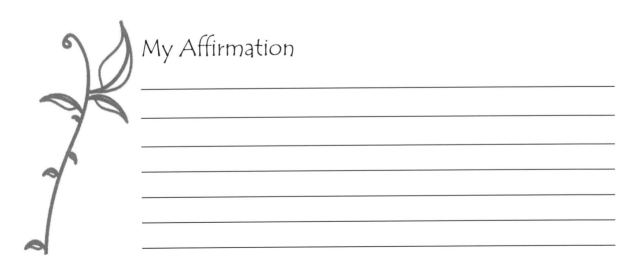

My Affirmation

_____

_____

_____

_____

_____

_____

My Reflections

Amazing, Brilliant, Compassionate YOU!

Remaining Charitable

A dreamer may not have a
paved road to travel.

At times there may be weeds of misunderstanding
that seem to grow into bushes of unkindness.

Though wounded with the words and fearful
thoughts of others, a dreamer remains charitable
and kind.

Walking with purpose and hope, a dreamer
embraces patience; learns to have undaunted faith
and heals always through love.

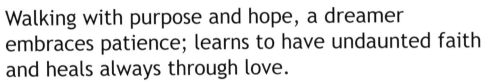

My Affirmation

_____

_____

_____

_____

_____

_____

My Reflections

_____

_____

_____

_____

_____

_____

_____

_____

_____

_____

_____

_____

_____

_____

_____

_____

_____

_____

_____

_____

_____

_____

_____

_____

_____

_____

_____

Amazing, Brilliant, Compassionate YOU!

Do Unto Others

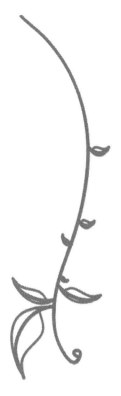

Often love is masked and hidden in our selfishness and need for control.

There are none among us who do not require love. A tree grows and a flower blossoms in love.

A dolphin sings and transmits sound waves of love. The air we breathe permeates love.

The good energy within the Universe is pure love.

All that we are when we become our best is love.

Dreamer, awaken to the power and breath of love.

All that you do, please do with love!!!!
Love and live!

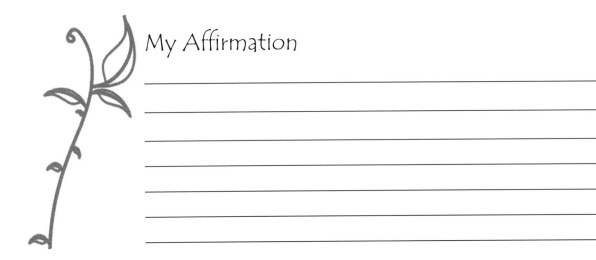

My Affirmation

_____

_____

_____

_____

_____

_____

My Reflections

Amazing, Brilliant, Compassionate YOU!

Life Upside Down

While Familiar has offered boundaries and a safe existence, the voice and feeling of Love will often turn your life upside down.

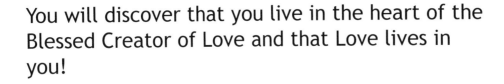

Unselfish Love is expansive
and unpredictable.

This Love will show you the nuances of Grace Everlasting and inspire you to want to share more of yourself, in ways you never shared before.

You will discover that you live in the heart of the Blessed Creator of Love and that Love lives in you!

Today, let Love turn you upside down so you can look at life from the Inside — Out!

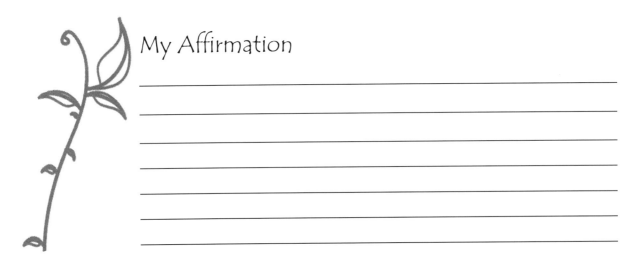

My Affirmation

_____

_____

_____

_____

_____

_____

My Reflections

Amazing, Brilliant, Compassionate YOU!

Met By Faith

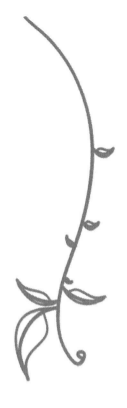

Every Seeker Dreamer knows that there has, and will be pain and disappointment in life.

Still, having learned the Power of Love, they walk with Compassion and learn to allow Forgiveness to heal their hearts over time.

This is the way that old sorrowful memories leave with the wind.

Only the memory of a difficult challenge met by Faith, nurtured by Love and offering new Hope remain. Joy, too, is ever present.

When we awaken and offer our Gratitude, A new day is always met by Faith, nurtured by Love; and offers new possibility with the vision of Hope.

My Affirmation

_____

_____

_____

_____

_____

_____

_____

My Reflections

Amazing, Brilliant, Compassionate YOU!

Aha Cha Cha!

Compassionate Love starts as a seed that dreams and becomes a thought that grows into a feeling shared by the Heart of the Uni-Verse.

Love flows like water in every act where you show you care.

Love moves through the air bringing rhythms of joy when you share.

It causes men to feel like boys and women to feel like girls as together they joyfully dance with the innocence and wonder of Love.

Aha, Cha Cha! Aha, Cha Cha! Aha, Cha Cha!
Turn, Whooooo! It's Love!
Aha, Cha Cha! Turn, Whooooo! It's Love!
Aha, Cha Cha, It's Love!
Aha Cha Cha, It's LOVE!

Integrity and Courage

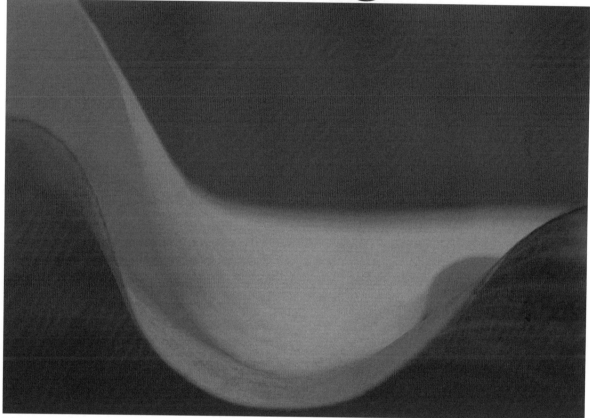

Photo: Bell Flower by Tyrone Rasheed

Right Words

A dreamer learns to silence the words of ego that harm and replace them with thoughts and words of compassion; even when another has wounded us! Right thoughts, right words and right actions of love transforms hearts and make more good possible!

Amazing, Brilliant, Compassionate YOU!

Divine Calling

A dreamer may have traveled far from their beginnings and achieved comfort and success only to wake up and discover they have more work to do.

With courage a dreamer remembers the Divine Calling and prepares to once again to take the next step into their unknown good destiny!

My Affirmation

_____

_____

_____

_____

_____

_____

My Reflections

Amazing, Brilliant, Compassionate YOU!

Fortitude

Though the Storms of life seemed wicked and unrelenting and the dreamer lost much, after the Storms subside one great thing remained:

Some call it Faith.

The Dreamer smiled joyfully because he and others were Still Alive.

If you have awakened today with a rainbow of integrity in your heart, then you too are Still Alive.

Be a Dreamer!
Feel the Power of Faith.

Give Thanks!
Use your gifts for Good!

Walk with Unrelenting Fortitude and Courage.

Begin to build the world you want your children to inherit!

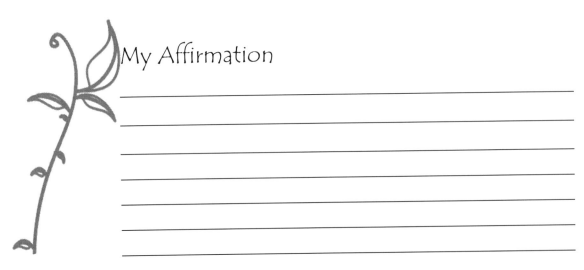

My Affirmation

_____

_____

_____

_____

_____

_____

_____

My Reflections

Amazing, Brilliant, Compassionate YOU!

I Will Do No Harm

Our fearful thoughts and careless actions can intercept the Blessings of Grace meant for us to grow in Love.

When this happens, our words become like swords that inflict wounds and deflate dreams.

Today, I will do no harm.

I Breathe Deeply and honor this understanding.

Ten times I Breathe.

In, Trust and Love.
Out, Tender Compassion.

I gently pay attention and open my heart so that Blessings of Grace and Love can move through.

I Breathe.
In Trust and Love.
Out Tender Compassion.
Today, I Will Do No Harm.

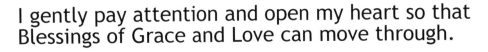 My Affirmation

_____

_____

_____

_____

_____

_____

_____

My Reflections

_____

_____

_____

_____

_____

_____

_____

_____

_____

_____

_____

_____

_____

_____

_____

_____

_____

_____

_____

_____

_____

_____

_____

_____

_____

_____

_____

_____

Amazing, Brilliant, Compassionate YOU!

The Greed Temptation

A dreamer will meet many who will try to woo you into the abyss of lost integrity.

The demon Greed may manifest, tempting you with riches laced in someone else's misfortune.

Greed caters to the selfish ego; teaches disregard of humanity, and tries to manipulate your good heart.

Everything you have and every thing you are is a gift from our Creator. Try to be diligent in Good.

Dreamer, use your gifts to serve and share!

Embrace the wisdom of your loving compassionate heart!

My Affirmation

_____

_____

_____

_____

_____

_____

My Reflections

_____

_____

_____

_____

_____

_____

_____

_____

_____

_____

_____

_____

_____

_____

_____

_____

_____

_____

_____

_____

_____

_____

_____

_____

_____

Amazing, Brilliant, Compassionate YOU!

Opening Doors

A dreamer may experience self-doubt. The dreamer asked this question when Confidence came to visit:

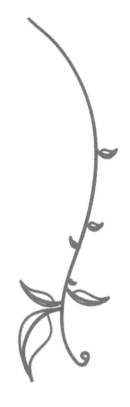

"What makes one continue to believe when doors keep closing?"

"All doors are not meant to be opened. Look for Respect and Faith." answered Confidence.

"You must Respect yourself, just as you respect others. Ask for Faith to guide you in goodness so that you use Intuition and learn to open the right doors!"

My Affirmation

_____

_____

_____

_____

_____

_____

_____

My Reflections

Amazing, Brilliant, Compassionate YOU!

How Do You Live

What we need to learn and teach is Purpose.

With Purpose we learn to be responsible for our every action!

A Dreamer who believes that their gifts and talents are to be shared for a Good Purpose grows and flourishes.

They learn to walk in Unity with Divine Spirit; pursue a path of excellence that benefits many; and bring more Joy to the world!

How Do You Live and Honor Good Purpose?

My Affirmation

_____

_____

_____

_____

_____

_____

_____

My Reflections

Amazing, Brilliant, Compassionate YOU!

Balance Requires Risk

Life will often ask us to risk the familiar so that space is created in Faith to embrace emotional integrity with clear vision.

The gift of balance is offered through our willingness to let go with a trusting heart.

At varying times, balance may require great risk which ultimately unfolds and blossoms in a Nurturing, Eternal Love born of Grace and Wisdom!

My Affirmation

_____

_____

_____

_____

_____

_____

_____

My Reflections

_____

_____

_____

_____

_____

_____

_____

_____

_____

_____

_____

_____

_____

_____

_____

_____

_____

_____

_____

_____

_____

_____

_____

_____

Amazing, Brilliant, Compassionate YOU!

Just You Watch Me!

Children play, learn and teach each other with the dare of encouragement. *"Bet you can't!"*, and the other replies *"Just you watch me!"*.

Courage and Commitment often come with a dare we make to ourselves to live our purpose and believe our good dreams.

 I Breathe Deeply Six Times.

Today, As I listen to the dreams of others, I will move beyond the dare and offer Love and Encouragement to All.

And if anyone says I can not do something that I believe is possible; I will Breathe Deeply.

In my mind and my heart I will smile and think, *"Just You Watch Me!"*

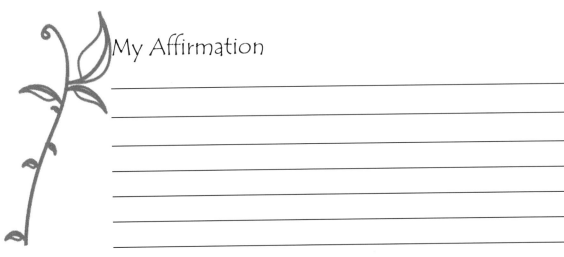 My Affirmation

_____

_____

_____

_____

_____

_____

My Reflections

A Peaceful Change Agent

Give thanks for another beautiful day!

Use your energy to uplift yourself and those around you to a higher vibration of love.

Speak and act kindly to each other, even in disagreement! Don't follow the crowd into a fire of despair and wrong actions.

Join those whose hearts lovingly work to bring good change!

Today, dreamer, be a peaceful change agent!

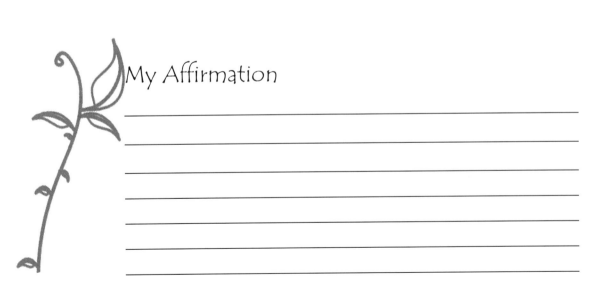

My Affirmation

_____

_____

_____

_____

_____

_____

My Reflections

Amazing, Brilliant, Compassionate YOU!

Joy and Sorrow

When we lose our jobs, or our homes; when we learn that we are ill and can not be cured; or when we say our final goodbyes to a Loved One — we discover what it feels like to be broken. Sorrow is forever knocking at our door.

How do we pick up the pieces of our broken lives? We open the door to Love.

With Love will come dear, old friends Compassion and Mercy. They are like sunshine to the clouds of Sorrow. And then, there are the tender moments and times of forgiveness and healing that bring the Rainbow of Joy. Rarely in life does one travel without the other.

Today, Breathe Deeply at least 10 Times. Even when Sorrow comes, Joy is ever-present to see us through the difficult times; and hold us tenderly with Love! We too must try always to offer Compassion and Mercy.

My Affirmation

_____

_____

_____

_____

_____

_____

_____

My Reflections

_____

_____

_____

_____

_____

_____

_____

_____

_____

_____

_____

_____

_____

_____

_____

_____

_____

_____

_____

_____

_____

_____

_____

_____

_____

_____

_____

_____

_____

Amazing, Brilliant, Compassionate YOU!

Desiring To Heal

Rejoice, Dreamer, Rejoice!

Rejoice and give thanks for this new day of mystery. Be grateful for the lessons of yesterday.

Embrace a sense of renewed purpose with confidence and hope. Breathe deeply and feel the gentle wisdom in your heart.

As you walk into the mystery of the new day, know that Spirit will guide you in every loving, compassionate step.

Rejoice, Dreamer, Rejoice!

Amazing, Brilliant, Compassionate YOU!

A Decision to Heal

The Seeker thought of the days past and breathed deeply four times; feeling and hearing the wisdom voice of the heart.

"If you knew me, then you would know my questions are meant to benefit, nurture and enrich your Spirit Energy so that your Soul is able to receive and transmit the message of cooperative understanding and Love."

~ * ~

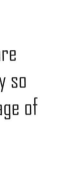

I Breathe In, the Mystery of the Creator's Song.
I Breathe Out, Love with Acceptance and
Cooperative Understanding.

We can be healed by our willingness to accept the Truth and build reconciliation through education, conversation, cooperative understanding and Love.

Ten Times I Breathe....
In, the Mystery of the Creator's Song and
Out, Love with Acceptance and
Cooperative Understanding.

My Affirmation

_____

_____

_____

_____

_____

_____

My Reflections

Amazing, Brilliant, Compassionate YOU!

Healing Oasis

No matter what others tell us the odds are, when we have the courage to embrace a difficult day and say *"I am ready"*, then peace will be the calling and answer of your heart.

Peace is a vibration filled with dignity and loving intent. Peace empowers you with faith and gives you the hope and strength you need to journey to the healing oasis.

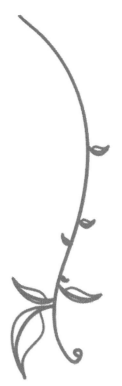

Even if it looks like we will fail in our efforts for peace, we must continue to believe that our efforts have value.

Success lies in our willingness to walk through the desert of despair and to keep sharing the love in our hearts ... ***no matter what!***

We will reach the oasis!

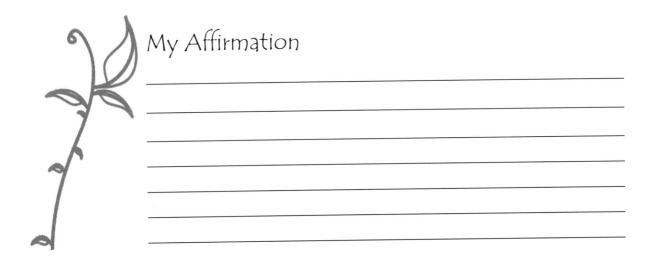

My Affirmation

_____

_____

_____

_____

_____

_____

My Reflections

Amazing, Brilliant, Compassionate YOU!

Shattered Pieces

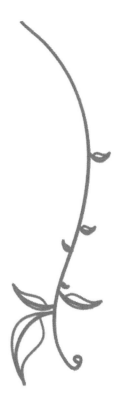

When the glass holding the water of my destiny shattered and broke … I stopped.

I stopped to pick up the pieces of broken promises and gently discarded them.

Now before I move on, I still myself:

I Breathe In the Oxygen of Love Eight Times.
I Exhale confusion and disappointment.

I recognize that the glass was too small a container to hold the water of my destiny.

No Glass Will Contain Me. Today, with Humility and Love; I Own My Good Destiny!

My Affirmation

_____

_____

_____

_____

_____

_____

My Reflections

Amazing, Brilliant, Compassionate YOU!

Your Beautiful Dream

A dreamer is one who steps out of their comfort zone and has chosen to embrace the magnet that draws whatever lessons you need closer to you.

When your heart is willing to accept and learn the lesson, you begin to experience peace within yourself.

Peace of mind on a difficult but rewarding journey brings new clarity and understanding to your beautiful dream.

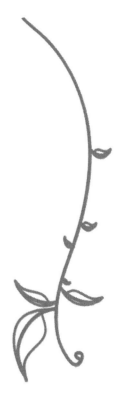

You will grow in strength, compassion
and new achievement!

My Affirmation

_____

_____

_____

_____

_____

_____

_____

My Reflections

_____

_____

_____

_____

_____

_____

_____

_____

_____

_____

_____

_____

_____

_____

_____

_____

_____

_____

_____

_____

_____

_____

_____

_____

_____

_____

_____

_____

Amazing, Brilliant, Compassionate YOU!

What I Want

Like many dreamers, I want to clear the weeds of old disappointment so I can feel the love of children as they play hide and seek among the trees or follow birds and butterflies across the meadow.

I want to meet you in the garden of Eternal Truth and offer the loving hope that resides somewhere hidden in my heart as I discover the place where Spirit lives in You.

I want a life beyond guns and war to be filled with Peace and Love on Our Precious Earth!

I want for myself and others ~ Healing!

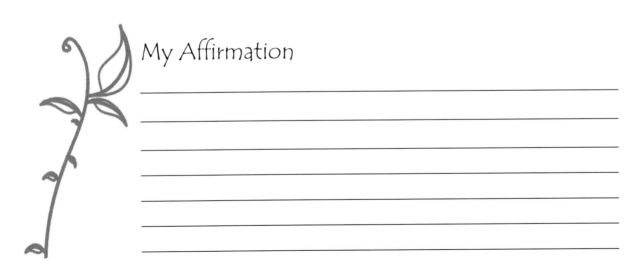

My Affirmation

_____

_____

_____

_____

_____

My Reflections

Amazing, Brilliant, Compassionate YOU!

Accepting Responsibility

On the day the rain poured with the wisdom of understanding, the dreamer offered prayers of gratitude with new appreciation.

This caused Patience and Courage to knock on her door of her heart. When the dreamer opened, they spoke in unison.

"It is time, time to accept responsibility
for your mistakes; to share your
light with respect for all;
and to sing Love's song of confidence
with a smile"

My Affirmation

_____
_____
_____
_____
_____
_____

My Reflections

Amazing, Brilliant, Compassionate YOU!

Rejoice Dreamer, Rejoice!

Rejoice and give thanks for this new day of mystery.

Be grateful for the lessons of yesterday.

Embrace a sense of renewed purpose with confidence and hope.

Breathe deeply and feel the gentle wisdom in your heart.

As you walk into the mystery of the new day, know that Spirit will guide you in every loving, compassionate step.

Rejoice, Dreamer, Rejoice!

My Affirmation

_____

_____

_____

_____

_____

_____

My Reflections

Amazing, Brilliant, Compassionate YOU!

Pray and Believe

A dreamer must pray not just for self but for others!

Believe that your prayers are being heard by the Divine Heart.

Walk as a giver and reflector of compassion.

Allow and believe that the good you want for yourself can be shared by others.

A dreamer believes that their prayers, gifts and good work will benefit many!

My Affirmation

_____

_____

_____

_____

_____

_____

My Reflections

_____
_____
_____
_____
_____
_____
_____
_____
_____
_____
_____
_____
_____
_____
_____
_____
_____
_____
_____
_____
_____
_____
_____
_____
_____
_____
_____

Amazing, Brilliant, Compassionate YOU!

Vision Quester

Every dreamer can become a Vision Quester when they journey inward to find the True Dream of Infinite Purpose residing within their heart.

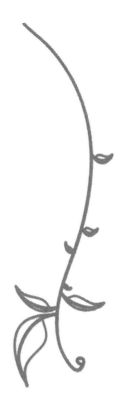

They first must let go of old habits and false perceptions they have about themselves.

Only then is the dreamer able to honor the deep insights of balance, clarity and strength needed to mobilize as the Vision Quester and move forward with loving intent!

My Affirmation

_____

_____

_____

_____

_____

_____

My Reflections

Amazing, Brilliant, Compassionate YOU!

I take a deep Breath and and then Breathe again.

I make a promise to myself.

I will learn to swim the rivers and oceans of unknowing.

I will climb the mountains of hope and walk across deserts of new understanding.

I will rest on beaches and reflect in the valleys.

I will allow the oasis of my heart to become renewed through my consistent discipline and good efforts to grow.

Humility

Receiving a Gift

No gift is too small. A dreamer must learn to honor the good intent of a giver, and to accept all gifts with sincere appreciation and gratitude.

No gift is too small when given with love!

Amazing, Brilliant, Compassionate YOU!

Right Words

A dreamer learns to silence the words
of ego that harm and replace them with
thoughts and words of compassion; even
when another has wounded us!

Right thoughts,
right words and right actions of love

... transforms hearts and make more good
possible!

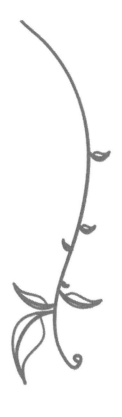

My Affirmation

_____

_____

_____

_____

_____

_____

My Reflections

_____

_____

_____

_____

_____

_____

_____

_____

_____

_____

_____

_____

_____

_____

_____

_____

_____

_____

_____

_____

_____

_____

_____

_____

_____

_____

_____

_____

_____

_____

_____

Amazing, Brilliant, Compassionate YOU!

Your Success

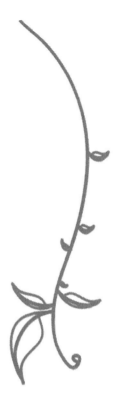

You may be excited and happy about a gift from our Blessed Creator.

Expect that your joy may not be shared by All. A dreamer's success often represents a lost dream for a family member or friend.

What you have accomplished may remind them of what they did not achieve.

Be patient and understanding. Allow your heart to be humble and kind. Walk with Gratitude.

Continue your journey and share hope with all!

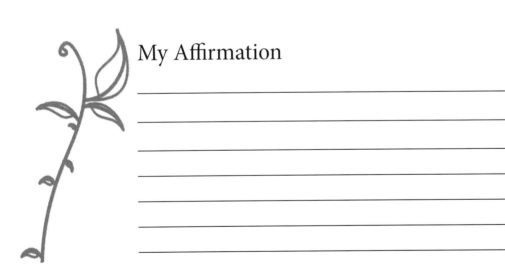

My Affirmation

_____

_____

_____

_____

_____

_____

My Reflections

Amazing, Brilliant, Compassionate YOU!

Divine Whisper

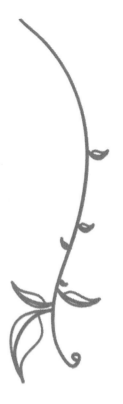

The Seeker Dreamer awoke to a Gentle Divine Whisper.

"Feel Me through your Tears. Know Me even in your Brokeness. Accept Me in Forgiveness. I AM Mercy.

I AM the Hope Blossoming in You! Today and every day, I AM the Answer. I live within YOU.

I feel through YOU. I Am the tingling strength you develop in wisdom and compassion.

Allow Me the Gift of Awakening within your heart and You Will See Me in every Tender Smile.

I AM the Answer. I AM LOVE!"

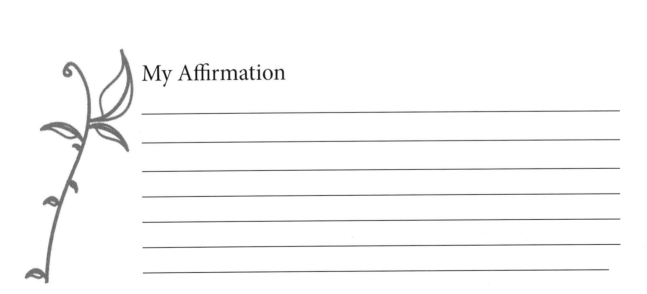

My Affirmation

_____

_____

_____

_____

_____

_____

My Reflections

Amazing, Brilliant, Compassionate YOU!

Possibility

Everything had shifted, and the dreamer believed that Love was every present.

Together, Confidence and Possibility went into the dreamer's heart.

The corridor's were many but they took each step with care and smiled when they felt the dreamer put on **Cloak of Humility.**

Now it was time for the dream to journey into the mystery of Possibility with the light of Confidence!

My Affirmation

_____

_____

_____

_____

_____

_____

My Reflections

Amazing, Brilliant, Compassionate YOU!

Brute Force

Brute force is always temporary and never offers any long-term solution.

A Seeker Dreamer learns that understanding comes when we move beyond our bias to see the best in others and offer the best in ourselves.

Always offer respect.

Today, be gracious with your words and actions.

Your respect and tender graciousness will change hearts and open a new pathway for your good dreams to manifest!

My Affirmation

_____

_____

_____

_____

_____

_____

_____

My Reflections

_____

_____

_____

_____

_____

_____

_____

_____

_____

_____

_____

_____

_____

_____

_____

_____

_____

_____

_____

_____

_____

_____

_____

_____

_____

_____

_____

_____

_____

Amazing, Brilliant, Compassionate YOU!

Is It The Ego?

Sometimes we must ask Ourselves,

> "Is it the ego needing a new victory
> or the heart asking you to Live in Truth?".

In all ways and all things seek Clarity. Breathe Deeply Eight Times With Gratitude for Your Life.

> Inhale Honesty, Perseverance and Faith.
> Exhale Humility with Self-Confidence and Love.
> Listen to your heart. Care fully.

Breathe Deeply Four Times. In all ways and all things seek Clarity.

> Inhale Honesty, Perseverance and Faith.
> Exhale Humility with Self-Confidence and Love.

Walk and Speak Gently!

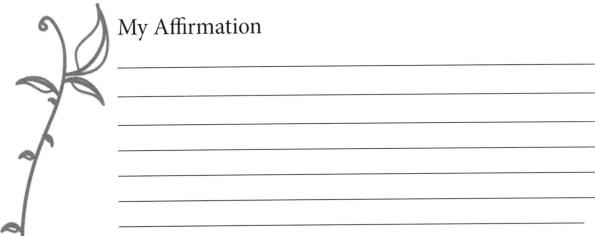

My Affirmation

_____

_____

_____

_____

_____

_____

My Reflections

Amazing, Brilliant, Compassionate YOU!

On Disagreement

When it's hot and steamy with disagreement, put on a cool suit of Respect and Be the Peace you desire.

An Affirmation—Today, I walk with Peace in my mind and my heart. I Am the Peace. In every steamy situation or disagreement ...

I stop.
I Breathe.
I listen deeply.

As I seek understanding, I remember to offer my respect generously. I say in my heart *"I Am the Peace"*.

I Give Thanks.
I Breathe.
I move forward firmly with a tender heart, listening deeply and offering respect for All.

My Affirmation

_____

_____

_____

_____

_____

_____

My Reflections

Amazing, Brilliant, Compassionate YOU!

Murky Waters

Though society does not always value Humility, every Wise Seeker has learned that Humility is a loyal friend and not adversary.

Dreamer, when you walk with Humility, Courage, Patience and Faith, your vision and deep desire to live a life of integrity will become like a clear reflection pond even in murky waters!

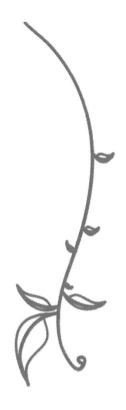

My Affirmation

_____

_____

_____

_____

_____

_____

My Reflections

Amazing, Brilliant, Compassionate YOU!

Bring Hope

In a world that sometimes appears dismal with lack of values and respect, every act of integrity kindness and valour still brings hope and nurtures the gardens of our hearts with good!

I Breathe Deeply Four times,
In, Integrity.
Out, Kindness.
With each breath, I allow my heart to open with Respect.
I Breathe again, and again.

With clarity, I commit to allow myself to be a vessel of Divine Peace so that my words and actions are able to be like the water of integrity and valour that flows, nurtures, and through Faith; brings Hope to Me, and All whose lives I touch! Slowly, I Breathe!

My Affirmation

_____

_____

_____

_____

_____

_____

My Reflections

Amazing, Brilliant, Compassionate YOU!

Engaging in Restoration and Transformation

The truth is ...
nothing will ever be as it was.

If you have awakened, then it is a
beautiful day to say, "thank you!"

Move forward, dream and believe
in the power of goodness!

You will become a catalyst when
you let go of old fears that have
anchored your heart.

Confidence

The Seeker Dreamer is like the Rising Sun that meets and embraces Moon at daybreak.

In this Heavenly exchange, The Seeker Dreamer awakens - carrying the wisdom learned through honoring and accepting the responsibility to have confide in oneself.

Today be like the Rising Sun.

Choose to have Confidence.

Trust the Wisdom of Your Heart!

My Affirmation

_____

_____

_____

_____

_____

_____

My Reflections

Amazing, Brilliant, Compassionate YOU!

What If ...

Some of us living with the pain of defeat often ask the question *"What IF?"*

What IF becomes a code word for *Don't Grow and Don't Change*.

The Phoenix Dreamer knows the code but approaches it with childlike curiosity. He looks sideways and sees other dreamers turning back. He looks back and sees his old self begging for him to return. He looks forward into the trees as they bow and honor the Sun. He feels the Wind of Chance.

He lets go and without halting - moves forward. If there is a stumble or fall, He gets up with the help of Desire and Confidence while Faith pushes Phoenix Dreamer forward.

Together they soar into the
Winds of Divine Chance!

My Affirmation

_____

_____

_____

_____

_____

_____

My Reflections

Amazing, Brilliant, Compassionate YOU!

Something New!

The truth is, nothing will ever be as it was.

If you have awakened, then it is a beautiful day to say thank you! Move forward, dream and believe in the power of goodness!

You will become a catalyst when you let go of old fears that have anchored your heart.

Today, have faith in your goodness potential.

Share your hope with love.

All is possible if you believe and honor the soul calling of Divine Spirit.

Begin today, and know without a doubt — *it is time for something new!*

My Affirmation

_____

_____

_____

_____

_____

_____

My Reflections

Amazing, Brilliant, Compassionate YOU!

How Do You Live?

I am learning to live like a Camel ... traveling peacefully through the deserts of evil in uncertain times.

Love is like the water stored in me.

It is Love that helps me regenerate my heart with Clarity and Truth as I follow the Master Creator's Phoenix of Hope and move across the sands of time to Heaven's Oasis.

I live like a Camel traveling peacefully through deserts of evil; nurtured and sustained by the Waters of LOVE!

How Do You Live?

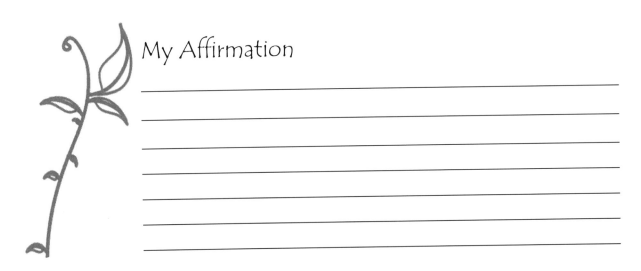

My Affirmation

_____

_____

_____

_____

_____

_____

My Reflections

_____

_____

_____

_____

_____

_____

_____

_____

_____

_____

_____

_____

_____

_____

_____

_____

_____

_____

_____

_____

_____

_____

_____

_____

_____

_____

_____

_____

Amazing, Brilliant, Compassionate YOU!

Re-Birth and Renewal

With Humility, I take a moment to still myself.

I Breathe Six Times and feel
the Love of the Uni-Verse embrace me
and offer the Grace of Renewal.
Deeply, I Exhale with each breath
and let go of every thought that is not Love.
I Breathe and offer Gratitude.
I open my heart and feel the lessons
of the dove, the dolphin, the butterfly
and the phoenix.

It is like I am walking on water into the clouds of Heaven. I am reminded that Wisdom offers Patience and Fluidity. Love's beginnings are beyond time and serve as an infinite Ocean of Grace that teaches Compassion. Love is meant to flow and has ending.

I Breathe and Exhale Deeply.
Only Through Love am I offered
Re-Birth and Renewal.
I Breathe with Gratitude!

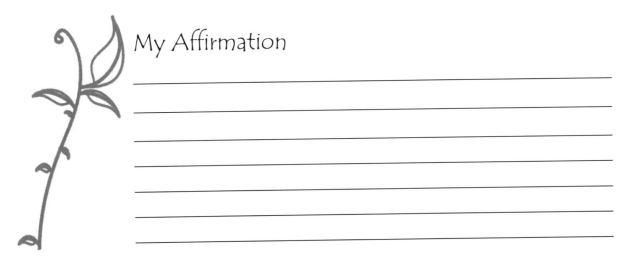

My Affirmation

_____

_____

_____

_____

_____

_____

My Reflections

_____

_____

_____

_____

_____

_____

_____

_____

_____

_____

_____

_____

_____

_____

_____

_____

_____

_____

_____

_____

_____

_____

_____

_____

_____

_____

_____

Amazing, Brilliant, Compassionate YOU!

Phoenix

When we let go of that which is complete and no longer needed in our lives, we are able to change and become more of who we are in our hearts.

A Phoenix can rise from the ashes of sorrow through gratitude, and with hope and purpose!

Breathe Deeply four times and honor the sorrowful change.

Now, feel gratitude for even the abrupt endings. Prepare and balance your heart with flexibility and hope.

Breathe slowly and deeply.

Today, remember this---
You Are like the Phoenix of Integrity and Truth rising with clear vision and a passionate heart.

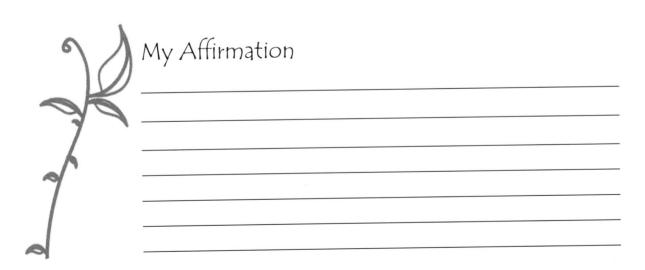

My Affirmation

_____

_____

_____

_____

_____

_____

My Reflections

Amazing, Brilliant, Compassionate YOU!

Joy and Spiritual Healing

The Journey to Love was long and arduous.

For the dreamer, every step forward seemed to be wed with a setback.

People said his hope was a foolish dream, still Hope was a constant companion.

Wisdom and Patience led the way.

Faith and Mercy stayed with him. They offered Spiritual Healing for every hurt.

When the dreamer met Joy in himself, like a Phoenix, the dream of Love was re-born over and over!

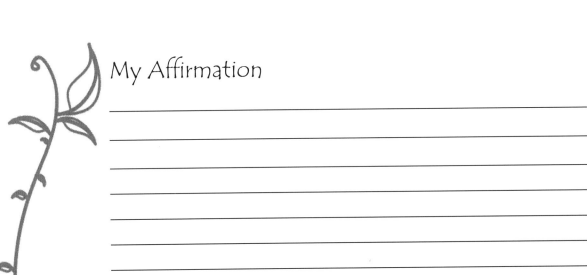

My Affirmation

_____

_____

_____

_____

_____

_____

My Reflections

Amazing, Brilliant, Compassionate YOU!

Love Has Many Roads

We may walk, ride a bike or take the bus. Some drive a car, row a boat or sail on the ocean. Others travel mostly by train and plane.

No matter our culture or religion; no matter what country you live in, some things about this world are truly the same.

There will be rains of kindness, storms of difficulty and lessons of Awakening to the Love. Through Love, we learn to let go of anger or fear.

We can embrace our power to heal, forgive, share and walk as Beings infused with the Creator's Grace!

Breathe Deeply Four Times.
Allow each breathe to be filled with Love.

Today, re-member that Love Has Many Roads and Desires only to be Awakened in Every Heart so that All may live and know the Sunshine of Hope!

 My Affirmation

_____

_____

_____

_____

_____

_____

My Reflections

Amazing, Brilliant, Compassionate YOU!

When Transformation Begins

Seeker Dreamer, when you become aware of the Song of love soaring throughout the Uni-Verse, a dreamer learns not to doubt the power or wisdom of our Mother Father Master Creator.

Faith filled with hope are ever present; creating beautiful images of joy even in our war-torn world.

Transformation begins when we look within our hearts and outside our doors of personal limitation!

We can choose to build new bridges of hope and forgiveness when we decide to sing and live the Song of Love!

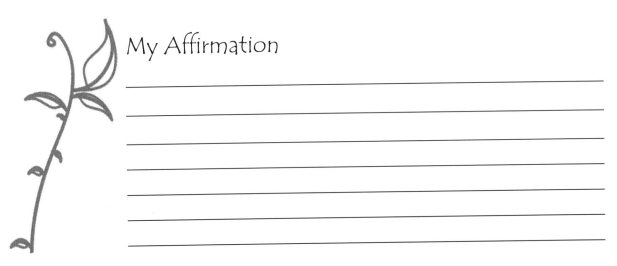

My Affirmation

_____

_____

_____

_____

_____

_____

My Reflections

_____

_____

_____

_____

_____

_____

_____

_____

_____

_____

_____

_____

_____

_____

_____

_____

_____

_____

_____

_____

_____

_____

_____

_____

_____

_____

_____

_____

Amazing, Brilliant, Compassionate YOU!

You Are A Miracle

Breathe Deeply In and Out Ten Times.
Remember Why You Are Here!

You are a Miracle; here to experience the beauty of Our Mother Earth; to sing with the birds, and learn from the trees as they share oxygen so you can breathe.

You are like a caterpillar who embraces the courage to transform into a beautiful butterfly. You are here to offer your talent and gifts of compassion; just as the bee offers honey for healing.

You are here to befriend your world neighbors while learning to live in Peace as you honor the oceans and rivers so that clean water is available to drink.

You willingly choose to nurture our Universal Sentient Family for Future Generations. There are so very many good reasons why you exist.

Seeker Dreamer, You, Are A Miracle.
Here to Grow and Prosper With A Loving Heart!
Breathe Deeply and Give Thanks!

My Affirmation

_____

_____

_____

_____

_____

_____

_____

My Reflections

Amazing, Brilliant, Compassionate YOU!

Star of Optimism

Every person living with Optimism shines like a Star and re-members to share the goodness of their heart.

Breathe Deeply Four Times.
In and Out.
Feel the Oxygen of Optimism enter your heart.

Affirm your path.

"I will patiently work to be consistent in my efforts to grow as I further develop my gifts. I will share the goodness of my heart and allow the Star of Optimism to guide me!"

Breathe Deeply Four Times.

Seeker Dreamer, Go Forth and Shine!

My Affirmation

_____

_____

_____

_____

_____

_____

My Reflections

When Dreamers Ring the Bells of Freedom and Unity

50TH ANNIVERSARY OF THE MARCH ON WASHINGTON

First Ever Civil Rights Foot Soldiers Memorial in Annapolis, Maryland.

When Will Freedom Come: Remembering the Civil Rights Foot Soldiers As Dreamers

by Reverend Melony McGant

Written for the Dr. Martin Luther King, Jr. Committee, Inc., in Celebration of the 50th Anniversary of the March on Washington and the Dedication of the CIVIL RIGHTS FOOT SOLDIERS MEMORIAL on August 28th, 2013 at 10:00AM, Whitmore Park in Annapolis, Maryland

There is perhaps no greater gift to society than the Dreamer.
For it is the Dreamer who believes that positive change is possible.
It is the Dreamer that looks upon a society's inequities
and desires a better life for themselves, their families,
their neighbors and their Nation.

It is the Dreamer who having awakened to the truth that
ALL people are created equal asks How Will Freedom Come?

On August 28th in 1963, A. Phillip Randolph, Bayard Rustin, John Lewis, Mahalia Jackson, Peter, Paul and Mary, Bob Dylan, Leon Bibb, Odetta, Jackie Robinson, James Baldwin, Marlon Brando, Paul Newman, Harry Belafonte, Sammy Davis Jr., Ossie Davis, Ruby Dee, Diahann Carroll, Burt Lancaster, Dr. Benjamin Mays, Roy Wilkins, Dorothy Height, Malcolm X and Dr. Martin Luther King, Jr. were all in attendance with 250 thousand Dreamers from across America who gathered in Our Nation's Capitol to rally for jobs, the right to vote, desegregation and equality.

Some of these Dreamers had been working in their communities, cities and states for many generations to bring about positive change. They knew that just attending the March on Washington was an act of rebellion but more importantly, it was an Act of Faith that could bring change and hope for their children.

People of all nationalities, religious beliefs and colors rallied for change. They were clergy, union members, mechanics, postal workers, railroad workers, pullman porters, butlers, maids, police officers, doctors nurses, educators, college students and people from every occupation imaginable.

Grandparents, mothers and fathers brought their children. Each of them believing that this country could demonstrate its greatness when Equality and Equal Opportunity became the law of the land.

It was Dr. Martin Luther King Jr. who spoke and articulated the Dream that had been swelling in the hearts of many for generations and generations.

Amazing, Brilliant, Compassionate YOU!

We know these 250,000 Dreamers as the Civil Rights Foot Soldiers. Though we may not know their names, today fifty year later, we honor the Civil Rights Foot Soldiers their lives, their hopes and their Dreams.

And fifty years later, the message of equality, equity, education, fair employment, hope and love continues to deserve our attention; for the work of the Dreamers and Civil Rights Foot Soldiers is far from complete.

Freedom will come only when we are willing to put down our guns;
open our hearts and listen deeply to Truth.
Freedom will come only when we
Rise Up Together
and decide to fix the broken
Political, Economic, Educational
and Social Systems of Inequity.

But Freedom Will Come!

As we remember The Civil Foot Rights Foot Soldiers, in our hearts, we will continue to walk across the nation with hope and strong resolve. We will hear, listen and sing the songs which commemorates our mourning for the loss of Every Child of War and Racism and Poverty. We will call for peace and sing of love.

Freedom will come when we truly desire Equity, Education and Prosperity For ALL. Freedom will come when we willingly sit at the table together in gratitude and share our dreams, our food, our homes, our education and our wealth.

Freedom will come when we once again notice that trees bend in reverence as Spring, Summer and Autumn Leaves dance joyfully and teach our children that all humans deserve to be cared for and loved!

Freedom will come as we re-member that for All Our Children, we must offer hope for their dreams and be willing to share our love.

Breathe Deeply
In, Hope. Out, Love.
Again Breathe.
In, Hope. Out, Love.

How will you honor the Dreamer Civil Rights Foot Soldiers?
Do you remember the Dream?
What will you do today and tomorrow?
How will Freedom come with Love and decide to Live in Our Hearts and Our Nation?

First, Breathe. In, Hope. Out, Love! We must once again commit to gather in our communities, cities and states. Remembering that ALL Are Created Equally, let us sit at the table together in Gratitude and share our Dreams, our food, our homes, our education and our wealth.

It is then Dreamer, that Freedom Will Come!

Amazing, Brilliant, Compassionate YOU!

Breathe and Remember:
The Civil Rights Foot Soldiers Memorial in
Annapolis and 50th Anniversary of the March on Washington

(c) Rev. Melony McGant

Beloveds,

If asked, "What do I remember about the Dreamer Civil Right Foot Soldiers and the 50th Anniversary of the March on Washington?", first I will Breathe Deeply Four Times. In Love. Out Good Change.

If asked, "what do I remember?", I will honor all those Dreamers who came before and ascended into the ethereal realm with hopes and dreams unfulfilled. I will remember each person should carry those hopes and dreams in their hearts.

I will say that I remember that America is a country where we have the right to gather together in our communities, our cities, our states and even our Nation's Capitol without being jailed or teargassed or shot by guns. We have the right to express our views and desire to actively work for Good Change.

I will remember that we must always have the Integrity to safeguard our Right to Vote and call for cessation of all violence and discrimination.

I will remember that our inalienable rights include good, equitable education, fair paying jobs, affordable healthcare and housing.

I will remember the good dreams of every child in America, the lost dreams and death of Trayvon Martin and the injust laws that promote violence and discrimination even today.

Today, and every day, I promise that I will honor the Dreamer Civil Rights Foot Soldiers by forming alliances in my heart with ALL, who like me, embrace Freedom, Integrity and a Desire to actively work for Good Change!

Now, Together, Let Us Breathe and Remember the Dreamer Civil Rights Foot Soldiers.

Breathe In Love.
Out Integrity and Hope.
And So It Is We Pray!

Testimonials from My Readers

"Melony is not what the world wants, she is what the world needs. Over the span of our one hour conversation, she changed my outlook on life. Her compassion is trumped only by the eloquence of her writing."
—Ian Aliman

"I have known Melony for just over 40 years and have seen her grow and blossom as a Flower of this Earth. With this growth has come knowledge and a special wisdom. Melony is truly a person of substance. She has great and wonderful passion for Life and all those who walk with Grace within it. She has become a daily source of Energy and Understanding and helps me to achieve my Center. I have always been able to turn to something she has said or written to help guide me as I seek truth and beauty in this world. She is a Blessing. I not only recommend Melony, but I encourage one to reach out and consult with her as a Life Coach."
—James Aloway

"Delightful, up left, wonderful, helpful, loving, caring, soulful, flowing words. Thank You for all you do on Facebook!"
—Judy Brown

"I hear God best in the morning. That still, small voice whispers direction, hope and love to me in a way I can hear and understand early when there is little to distract me. How many mornings have I risen to affirmation of that direction, hope and love by way of Melony's beautiful, mindful words? Many. How many times have I revisited those words for comfort? Many. Simply: She's a blessing."
—Robin Caldwell

"Melony McGant is an incredible, compassionate and motivating woman that is full of life. She is a wonderful life coach with exceptional active listening and communication skills. Knowing Ms. McGant and reading her latest book has inspired me to live life to the fullest. I look forward in reading more of her books."
—Diane Chan

"Inspiration, salvation, courage, peace, joy, love, blessings, affirmation, confirmation, insight, perspective, encouragement, clarity, gratitude, everything!"
—Marilyn G. Charity

"Melony, I always look forward to your daily meditations. I like them because each one reminds me to pause whatever I am doing and take a few Breaths. I feel better when I pause and breathe. Your mediations are a very real Blessing ..."
—Mary Christopher

Testimonials from My Readers, cont.

"Ms. McGant's acquaintance has impacted my life from the moment we met. She is a caring, enthusiastic for life, truly invested upon her work individual. She assisted me in finding employment and has continued to offer her opinion and help in my professional development. I am truly blessed to have met Ms. McGant and continue to look forward to years of Ms. McGant's words and uplifting spirit."
—Sara DeJesus

"Fourteen years ago I wrote a children's book that brought me together with Melony at a booksigning event. During those early days of promoting my book, like Dickens wrote, it was "The best of times, it was the worst of times". I had never met Melony before the book signing, but with her special sensitivity that day, she felt the emotional pain I was going through and over the next several months Melony talked me off of "the ledge" and taught me to appreciate, not only the accomplishment of writing the book, but also taught me to appreciate who I really was and what I had to offer others.

Fast forward to last summer when I almost "checked out" from something called "flash pulmonary edema". Without getting too technical, it involves retaining CO_2 instead of breathing it out. It is no accident that I started to really tune into Melony's daily messages about breathing exercises that also included beautiful messages of love, compassion, creativity, forgiveness, generosity, awakening to all that was good and glorious about life and living and sharing and caring, and so on and so on and so on. Melony's gifts can now be experienced by all with her new book, a book that will give all the exercises needed to fulfill ones dreams, to absorb all the beautiful things that we should experience during our time here and now."
—Vincent Esoldi

"Melony is the inspirational voice to help other people reclaim the power to heal themselves physically, emotionally, and spiritually. Her efforts are sincere in helping people to grow and heal thru their life transitions. Our acquaintance has been a significant healing catalyst in my own personal journey. She coached me into transforming and energizing my mind and spirit, as a result I healed my environment by changing my residence and career. I have never been at a more happier or peaceful state of mind as I am now! She exudes a natural sincere healing energy that resonates with you on a deep level. She is captivating and empowering."
—Venus Firebird

"Melony, I have enjoyed your works over the years because they have allowed me to witness your growth as a writer"
—Charles E. Greene II

"Melony McGant is a dynamic individual and a motivational thought leader. She is a talented writer with boundless energy who has an exceptional skill for inspiring others. Melony is incredibly compassionate and has assisted many folks from various backgrounds in meaningful and substantial ways. I know she takes personal delight in helping and inspiring others in a positive ways. I highly recommend her and her work."
—Sunil Gupta

Amazing, Brilliant, Compassionate YOU!

Testimonials from My Readers, cont.

"When I first met Melony I was immediately drawn to her remarkable spirit as a human being. Secondly, her compassion to help people in their everyday lives. She has the ability to uplift thousands of readers with her prolific style of writing on her daily blogs. Melony has various high leveled skills in the field of marketing and branding. I can account that she is a woman of great integrity and professionalism."
—Joe James

"Waking up to Melony's wisdom means that I immediately become aware. It is uncanny how many times Melony's message serendipitously seemed written just for me. Her messages mean balance, calmness, peace, beauty, spirituality, divinity and sisterhood! Namaste!"
—Yvette Jarvis

"I thought I was alone. I felt afraid. I closed my eyes to pray and dared to dream. I felt encouraged and renewed. I could hear a small gentle voice whispering take 3 deep cleansing breaths, let the Spirit in. Now share it. I'm not alone and the world is not such a big place. This is your daily reminder to me...Stay Blessed!"
—Sandra McEwen Gilbert-Blair

"Whenever I get so bored or troubled by the many challenges that my nation is facing, I read through your Facebook posts on the Inter-religious Ambassadors Group and do the exercises. I get relieved and refreshed to begin life anew. Yours have been so inspiring and rewarding but many seem not to understand this approach of doing it for yourself and not having someone do for you."
— Raphael Ogar Oko

"I am always reminded the way things should be done positively when Melony writes. She's one who is sharing God, love, peace, joy, happiness and wisdom from her heart and soul. She is leading the way preaching, serving our people spiritually, to all of those who will listen. She speaks about the many treasures one should know. Her way is the gentle way, yet an easy understanding way. Nothing complicated, easy to endure.

Melony begins being thankful with gratitude for waking up mornings, not to forget the breath we need to take. The mother-earth to me is her favorite to speak about, giving peace, trust and love, not to forget its beauty. Always to mention about giving someone you don't know a friendly smile, some help or a hug. We can truthfully use a whole lot more of finding hope. She is a great example for us all. She is a positive inspiration with dedication. Namaste!"
—Joe (Blow) Robinson

Testimonials from My Readers, cont.

"This a wonderful person, an enlightened soul, and my friend, Melony, she starts each day by filling our hearts, our souls, and our minds, with wisdom, compassion, and love. And I think today, you need her. "
—Christopher A. Sanchez

"Melony, I just want to say that there are certain things I look forward to doing each new day. I look forward to waking to the new day, having done that, I look forward to expressing my gratitude via my morning prayer. Occasionally, I'll eat a little breakfast, and then, I check to see what you've written to inspire us that day. There have been times when I've had to leave home early, too early to see what you've done. In cases like that I'll just go back to something you wrote before, and I'm good to go.

Without knowing it, you've eased my walk through a many day, for which I will be eternally grateful. You put the love back when it seems to have vanished. Your inspired words say it's okay to hope, to feel, to believe, and to move on. I thank you for that and I implore you, please, keep on keeping on."
—Jim Willis

"Melony, I enjoy your inspirational words and breathing techniques. It is a great way to help people bring about positive change in their lives. Learning how to breathe with intention allows you to connect lovingly with yourself, become balanced and retain a great deal of focus. Namaste!"
—Reverend Nettie Paisley

"Rev. Melony: Your daily meditations have been a source light and love to me. They are a constant reminder of the Spiritual essence of souls that seek to find acceptance, healing, peace, love and deliverance. Each one is a divine glow which collects vibrations of the supernatural "high" ways of God Almighty. May you continue to move within the calling of the Master, our Lord Jesus Christ. And may each meditation shine a light, radiating love in all those dark places."
—Elder Denise L. White

Amazing, Brilliant, Compassionate YOU!

About Melony

Melony McGant is a poet, humanist & compassionate communications professional with more than 20 years of experience in assisting both people and organizations discover and promote their professional or personal life missions. She has a strong track record of success in public relations, cause marketing, special events programming, and workshop facilitation.

She has received several awards and recognition for her volunteer and community efforts which include the Pittsburgh City Council Women's Recognition Award, the Minority Business Enterprise Legal Defense and Education Fund Community Service Award (MBELDEF), the New Mexico Not Even One Service Award, and the 911 Red Cross Volunteer Award.

Melony is an ordained Interfaith Minister, a professional storyteller and author.

Other publications from Melony:
"Sunshine & Olivier: A Parable of Love (IUniverse)"
"The Healing Adagio…A Love Symphony in Five Parts"

A member of the American Academy of Poets and the Poetry Society of America and the International Association of Coaches (IAC), her work included in several anthologies, including The Book of Hope and The World Book of Healing (both by Beyond Borders Press), and Go Tell Michelle: African American Women Write to Michelle Obama (SUNY Press).

To contact Melony McGant to speak or conduct a Seeker Dreamer Workshop email her at melonymcgant@yahoo.com

View her blog at www. melonymcgant.blogspot.com

Feel free to write her at:

Melony McGant
P.O. Box 230103
New York, NY 10023

Phone : 212-502-0895

For Review Copies Contact Author House 800-839-8640

Amazing, Brilliant, Compassionate YOU!

Unrelenting Love

Across the ethers of time forgotten,
through the winds of chance
unknowingly planned;
Destiny offers free will
and Love.

Love then, becomes both a choice
and a responsibility.

Traveling across the Uni-verse
swimming in the depth of oceans
feeling the breath of Love
that offers strength, courage
and hope that soothes
sorrow and offers forgiveness...

With joy, I am re-born through faith
always with the gift of
Unrelenting Love.

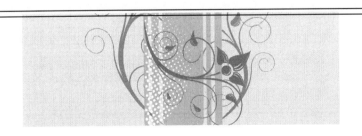

Made in the USA
San Bernardino, CA
02 February 2015